The Sound of Brushes

by

ED THIGPEN

Project Manager: Ray Brych
Cover Art: Odalis Soto
Engraver: Mark Young
Text Editor: Nadine DeMarco
Project Coordinator: Yoni Leviatan

INTRODUCTION

The use of brushes is not new. I have been told that as early as the 1920s the brushes were becoming an integral part of the drummers' equipment.

It would be impossible for any of us to develop without the influence of others. I would like to acknowledge some of the people who have had the greatest influence on my approach to playing brushes: my father Ben Thigpen, Jo Jones, Denzil Best, Art Blakey, Buddy Rich, Max Roach, Shelly Manne, and Elvin Jones. One cannot help but be influenced by these great artists.

Since the emergence of rock music, which for the most part requires heavy drumming, the brushes were set aside or, for most of the young players who began playing during this period, have never been used at all.

In 1965 I wrote a book entitled *Ed Thigpen Talking Drums* in which was included a few pages of diagrammed brush strokes. It was then suggested that I do a book totally devoted to brush technique.

This book is the result. All of the strokes included herein I use, depending upon the musical situation. It is my sincere hope that *The Sound of Brushes* will help you in developing effective brush technique.

ED THIGPEN

Renowned the world over for his exemplary musicianship, brush artistry, and acclaimed teaching methods, Ed Thigpen is considered by musicians and critics alike to be one of the finest drummers/percussionists in jazz.

Born December 28, 1930, in Chicago, Ed was raised, however, in Los Angeles where, while studying music with Samuel Brown, he acquired drumset experience with his school's swing band. In fact, his unwavering dedication and skills earned him the Thomas Jefferson High School music award.

In 1951 he moved to New York City and joined the Cootie Williams Band, playing at the Savoy Ballroom and later touring the U.S. with a number of well-known R&B performers.

Serving in the army between 1952 and 1954, Ed gained his initial experience as a drum instructor with the Sixth Army Band Training Unit before doing a tour of duty in Korea with the Eighth Army Band.

It was between the years 1954 and 1958 while working with such artists as Dinah Washington, Gil Mellé, Bud Powell, Jutta Hipp, and the Billy Taylor Trio that Ed laid the foundation for what has become one of the most enduring and respected careers in jazz. It was during the period with the Billy Taylor Trio and working on the TV series "The Subject Is Jazz" when he decided to pursue his concepts in jazz education.

Ed first gained worldwide acclaim through his work with Oscar Peterson and Ray Brown in what many still believe to be the greatest piano-bass-drums trio in the history of jazz. His contribution to this trio earned him the 1959 *Down Beat* critics' New Star Award. Ed's association with the trio lasted six and a half years (January 1959–June 1965).

In June 1966 he accepted an invitation to tour with the great jazz vocalist, Ella Fitzgerald, with whom he worked until January 1967. Ed then moved to Los Angeles where he became active in studio recording sessions as well as working with notable singers Pat Boone, Johnny Mathis, and Peggy Lee and the orchestras of Oliver Nelson and Gerald Wilson.

In 1968 Ed re-joined Ella Fitzgerald in a trio led by Tommy Flanagan. He remained with Ella and Tommy until September 1972, when he settled in his current home and base of operation, Copenhagen, Denmark. From there he has maintained a busy schedule of international performances with both European and American artists. Additionally, his role as an educator has continued to expand with teaching positions, the publication of several highly acclaimed method books and educational videos, as well as written articles and advisory contributions for *Modern Drummer* magazine, *The Jazz Educators Journal,* and the Percussive Arts Society. All of which further serve to underwrite the undeniable value of Ed Thigpen's continuing contributions to the art of jazz drumming—past, present, and future.

TABLE OF CONTENTS

SOUND OF BRUSHES - CD 1

Track 01 . . Introduction . . . .Sounds of Brushes
Track 02 . . Page 13 . . . . . . .Brush Strokes for Playing Time (Left Hand)
Track 03 . . Page 14 . . . . . . .Basic Right-Hand Ride Pattern
Track 04 . . Page 15 . . . . . . .Combined Basic Right- and Left-Hand Time Strokes
Track 05 . . Page 16–17 . . . .Phrasing in Time (Tempo) Explanation and Demo
Track 06 . . Page 18 . . . . . . .Right-Hand Punctuation — Basic Left-Hand Brush Sweep
Track 07 . . Page 18 . . . . . . .Demo. and Play-Along With Piano and Bass
Track 08 . . Page 19 . . . . . . .Left-Hand Punctuation
Track 09 . . Page 20 . . . . . . .Left-Hand Punctuation — Right-Hand Ride Rhythm
Track 10 . . Page 20 . . . . . . .Demo and Play-Along With Piano and Bass
Track 11 . . Page 21 . . . . . . .Accented Right Hand (on "let" count of first G.P. beat)
Track 12 . . Page 21 . . . . . . .Play-Along
Track 13 . . Page 22 . . . . . . .Accented Left Hand (on "let" count of first G.P. beat)
Track 14 . . Page 23 . . . . . . .Accented Right Hand (on "let" count of second G.P. beat)
Track 15 . . Page 24 . . . . . . .Accented Left Hand (on "let" count of second G.P. beat)
Track 16 . . Page 25 . . . . . . .Accented Right Hand (on "let" count of fourth G.P. beat)
Track 17 . . Page 26 . . . . . . .Accented Left Hand (on "let" count of fourth G.P. beat)
Track 18 . . Page 26 . . . . . . .Demo and Play-Along
Track 19 . . . . .Random Two-Bar Phrase Play-Along With Piano and Bass
Track 20 . . Page 27 . . . . . . .Basic Left-Hand Sweep With Right-Hand Tap-Tick Sound
Track 21 . . Page 28 . . . . . . .Left-Hand Half Circle
Track 22 . . Page 28 . . . . . . .Half-Circle Time Sweep: 2 Feel With Piano and Bass
Track 23 . . Page 29 . . . . . . .Left-Hand Full Circle (Instruction)
Track 24 . . Page 29 . . . . . . .Demo and Play-Along Left-Hand Full Circle With Piano and 4/4 Walking Bass
Track 25 . . Page 30 . . . . . . .Right-Hand Hook Stroke (Instruction)
Track 26 . . Page 30 . . . . . . .Demo and Play-Along With Piano and Bass
Track 27 . . Page 31 . . . . . . .Right-Hand Hook Stroke/Left-Hand Half Circle
Track 28 . . Page 31 . . . . . . .Demo and Play-Along (2 Feel)
Track 29 . . Page 32 . . . . . . .Left-Hand Full Circle/Right-Hand Hook Stroke
Track 30 . . Page 32 . . . . . . .Demo With Piano and 4/4 Walking Bass Line
Track 31 . . Pages 27–32 . . .Demo and Play-Along (2 Feel and 4/4 Walking Bass)
Track 32 . . Pages 27–32 . . .Play-Along for Ballad Strokes

SOUND OF BRUSHES - CD 2

Track 01 . . Page 33 . . . . . . .Right-Hand Zorro Stroke
Track 02 . . Page 34 . . . . . . .Right-Hand Zorro Stroke and Left-Hand Half Circle
Track 03 . . Page 34 . . . . . . .Demo and Play-Along
Track 04 . . Page 35 . . . . . . .Right-Hand Zorro Stroke With Left-Hand Full Circle
Track 05 . . Page 35 . . . . . . .Demo and Play-Along
Track 06 . . Page 35 . . . . . . .Play-Along Med to Fast Tempos
Track 07 . . . . .Play-Along Track Without Drums
Track 08 . . Page 37 . . . . . . .Basic Ride Rhythm in 3/4 Time
Track 09 . . Page 37 . . . . . . .Demo and Play-Along With Piano and Bass
Track 10 . . Page 38 . . . . . . .Accented "Let" Count of One in 3/4 Time
Track 11 . . Page 38 . . . . . . .Demo and Play-Along With Piano, Bass, and Voice
Track 12 . . Page 39 . . . . . . .Instruction of Sixteenth-Note Triplet Punctuation in 3/4 Time
Track 13 . . Page 40 . . . . . . .Sixteenth-Note Triplet Punctuation in 4/4 Time
Track 14 . . Page 41 . . . . . . .Stroke for Double-Time Feeling (Instruction)
Track 15 . . Page 41 . . . . . . .Demo and Play-Along
Track 16 . . . . .Bonus Track: Alternate Double-Time Feel, Zorro Stroke
Track 17 . . Page 41 . . . . . . .Demo and Play-Along
Track 18 . . . . .Random Play-Along Track for Double-Time Feeling
Track 19 . . Page 42 . . . . . . .Altered Triplet Shuffle (Instruction)
Track 20 . . Page 42 . . . . . . .Play-Along
Track 21 . . Page 43 . . . . . .Tight Shuffle Sweep (Instruction)
Track 22 . . Page 43 . . . . . . .Demo and Play-Along
Track 23 . . Pages 42, 43 . . .Play-Along for Shuffle Strokes
Track 24 . . Page 44 . . . . . . .Brush-Tap-Tick-Brush (Instruction)
Track 25 . . Page 44 . . . . . . .Short Play-Along
Track 26 . . Page 45 . . . . . . .Strumming — Guitar Stroke (Instruction)
Track 27 . . Page 45 . . . . . . .Short Play-Along
Track 28 . . Page 46 . . . . . . .Tap-Sweep-Tap Time Stroke (Instruction)
Track 29 . . Page 46 . . . . . . .Short Demo and Play-Along
Track 30 . . Page 47 . . . . . . .Dit-Dash, Dit-Dash, Dit-Dash
Track 31 . . Page 49 . . . . . . .Brush Strokes for Latin American Music (Instruction and Demo)
Track 32 . . Page 55 . . . . . . .Funk, R&B, Fusion Patterns (Instruction and Demo)
Track 33 . . Pages 55–58 . . .Demo and Play-Along — Slow Groove

The Brush

The wire brush is constructed with thin wires bound together in the shape of an open fan. There are different types of handles made, to which the brush is connected. Below are pictures of two types: one with a wood handle and the other with a hard aluminum shaft covered with a rubber sleeve.

Most models are made with an open shaft handle so that wires can be retracted into the handles for protection when not in use.

Plastic and nylon materials are also being used for making brushes and, as an alternative sound and feel source, are quite effective. As with sticks, the choice of the type of brush you use is a personal one.

I prefer a brush with thin, very flexible wires as my main brush. Nevertheless, I use stiffer wire and plastic/nylon types as sources for alternative sounds and feels as well.

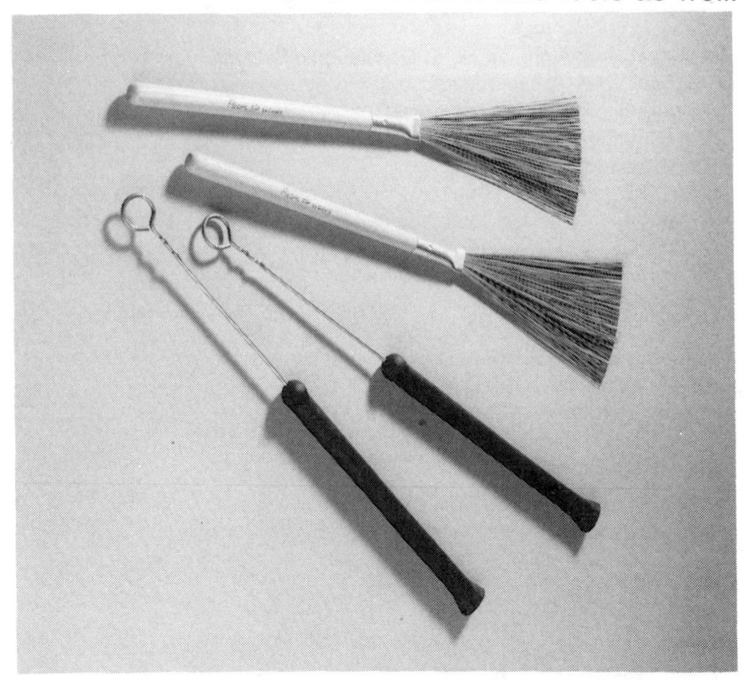

Brush Technique

Both sticks and brushes should be thought of as an extension of the hand when in use. The one difference is that the wires of the brush are flexible, whereas the stick remains rigid since it is made from a single piece of wood.

The flexibility of the brush affords us other effects and sounds that cannot be made with a stick. Because of the flex of the wires, an additional technique must be developed to get the maximum use from the brushes.

Grips for Playing Brushes

The brushes are held basically the same as the sticks. Either the conventional grip or the matched grip can be used. I use the conventional grip most of the time. I have found slight alterations in the position of the left hand necessary for some strokes. (This point will be mentioned when necessary on the instructional CDs.)

Brush Sounds and Rhythmic Feels

There is no standard notation or sign for a specific brush sound. When brushes are desired in an arrangement, the word "brushes" or initials "Br." or "W.B." are generally written in at the beginning of the section of the arrangement in which their use is desired. In most cases, it is up to the drummer to decide when the brushes will provide the best effect.

As a guide, I suggest you will be safe in using brushes whenever the music calls for very soft playing: *piano, pianissimo,* and so on. There are times, however, when brushes can be very effective in a *forte* (loud) dynamic range. The sound and special feeling the brushes generate is quite noticeable, particularly when they are being used to play a strong basic swing ride rhythm.

Six basic sounds will be applied when practicing the strokes and patterns illustrated in *The Sound of Brushes* book and on the accompanying CD: the "tick" sound, the "tap" sound, the "slap" or "flat" sound, and the "shhhhh," "brushhh," or "tchh" sounds.

I suggest you speak or sing each of these sounds vocally first and then try to duplicate your vocal sound with the brush on the drum or whatever surface on which you're playing. Good dynamic reference points to use for each of the sounds could be the following:

"tick" = soft, "tap" = medium-loud or "accented" (listen to these sounds on CD 1, Track 1)

Next , speak and/or sing "shhhhh," "swishh," and "brushhh," vocally demonstrated on CD 1, Track 1.

Rhythmic Feels

The style and rhythmic feel of music when played in tempo can be determined and executed by the use of two fundamental pulse beats: We will call these two basic pulse beats the *ground pulse* and its *dominant mini-pulse.*

The ground pulse is designated by the lower number in the time signature, for example:
/4 = quarter note G.P.   /8 = eighth note G.P.

The dominant mini-pulse can be any note or rest sign of a shorter duration than the G.P., for example:

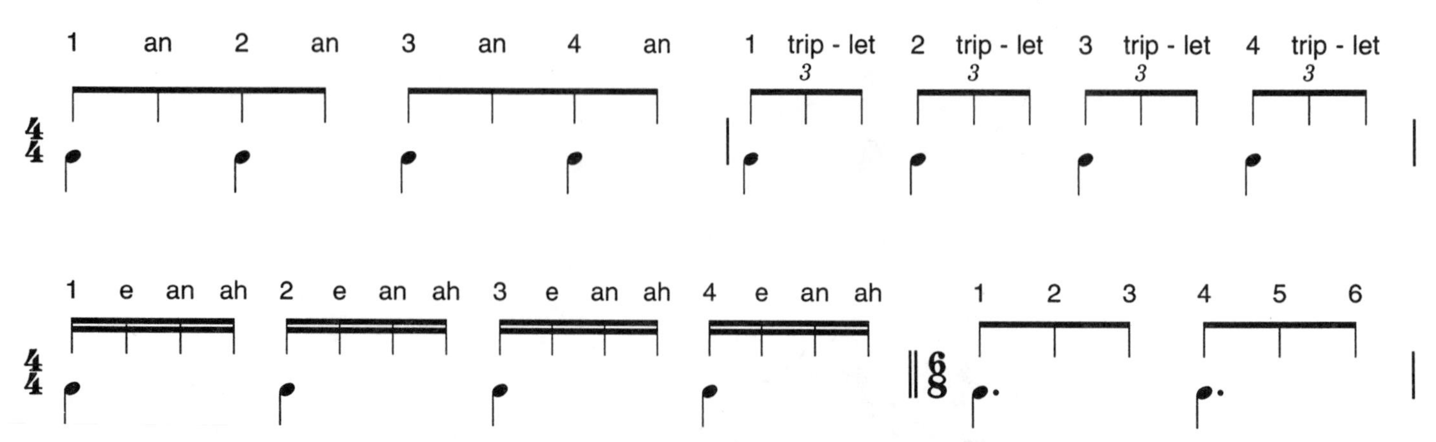

Rhythmic Feels/Ground Pulse and Mini-Pulse

Whereas all of the various notes, rest signs, or combinations of mini-pulse beats can be used to create various rhythms, the overall rhythmic interpretation of a musical style or segment of any music being performed can be determined by activating a basic ground pulse beat and its dominant mini-pulse simultaneously.

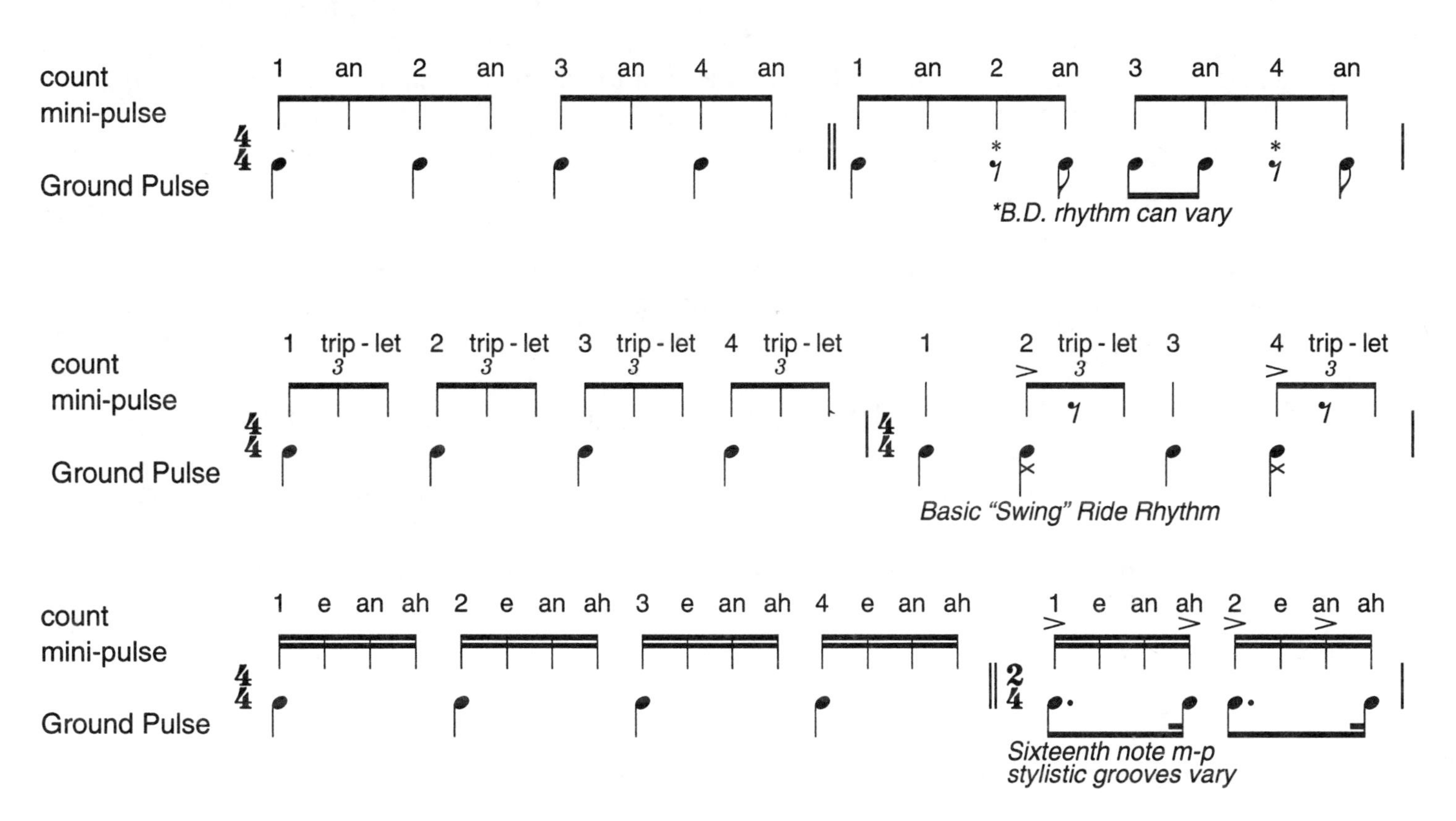

Tap the G.P. with your foot in a steady tempo. Count out the mini-pulse beats while tapping the ground pulse beat with your foot. Use a metronome or click track to check the steadiness of the G.P. foot tap.

These mini-pulse beats are always active whether sounded or not. They are expressed in the breathing and or vibrato of the instrumentalist or vocalist.

Recommended Study and Practice Procedure

In my teaching experience, I have found that many students, advanced as well as beginners, do not thoroughly read the written text included in most instruction books. Therefore, I ask you to please read the text in this book carefully. The same applies to listening: Please, listen to the recorded instructions and sounds of the various brush strokes on the CD carefully. Listen to each recorded track at least once or even twice before attempting to play along with it. Look at the illustrated diagrams and try to follow the instructed hand movements, visually first. Next, trace and/or tap out the rhythmic pattern of the illustrated diagrams with your finger tips only. The idea is to transfer the feeling of the strokes and patterns from your hands to and through the brushes. The brush should be thought of and felt as an extension of the hand—not a foreign object.

I also recommend that you practice all of the strokes accompanying yourself with a steady pulse on the bass drum and/or hi-hat. After you have practiced with the play-along tracks on *The Sound of Brushes* CD, try playing along with some recordings from your personal collection.

I highly recommend listening to and playing along with old and new recordings by jazz masters performing in various styles of this evolving music in both small and large ensemble settings, for instance, early blues, R&B, Dixieland, swing, and bebop. This can be a great help for becoming familiar with different jazz styles, which make full use of the eighth-note triplet mini-pulse, an important element in jazz interpretation. Listening to well-performed music can also help increase your song repertoire.

Ed Thigpen Selected Available Discography*

As Leader:
Out of the Storm — Verve/Polygram (Verve Master Edition)
Young Men and Olds — Timeless
Easy Flight — Reaction Records/Stunt (Re-issue)
Mr. Taste — Justin Time
It's Entertainment — Stunt Records

As Sideman:
Night Train — with Oscar Peterson — Verve/Polygram
Westside Story — with Oscar Peterson — Verve/Polygram
Ben Webster Meets Oscar Peterson — Verve Master Edition
Complete Set — London House Recordings — with Oscar Peterson — Verve
Jazz at Santa Monica Civic — with Ella Fitzgerald — Pablo

All of these CDs have excellent tracks on standard and original melodies that may also be used for play-along practice with the illustrated brush strokes. Songs on the recordings are played in medium to fast tempos, as well as slow to medium tempo ballads with grooves/feels, in 2/2, walking 4/4, 2 feel, and 3/4 time.

The rhythmic patterns and strokes illustrated in *The Sound of Brushes* will give you more than enough brush strokes to adapt to any style or situation where the use of brushes might be suitable.

* Remember! It is very, very important that you listen to a variety of recordings with different drummers using brushes in various musical settings. This will help you to develop your own taste and eventually your own style.

Sweep, Lift, and Tap Signs

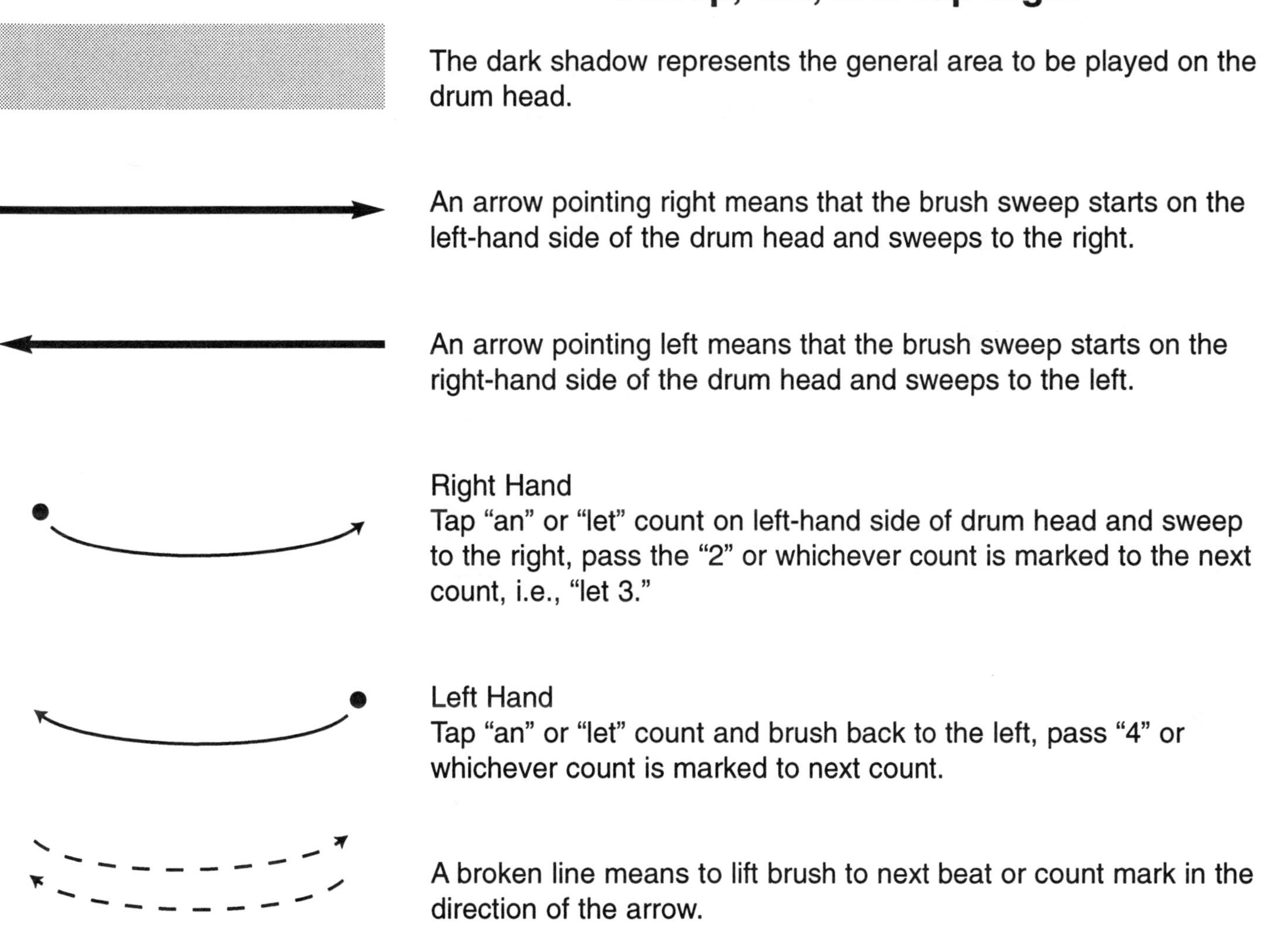

The dark shadow represents the general area to be played on the drum head.

An arrow pointing right means that the brush sweep starts on the left-hand side of the drum head and sweeps to the right.

An arrow pointing left means that the brush sweep starts on the right-hand side of the drum head and sweeps to the left.

Right Hand
Tap "an" or "let" count on left-hand side of drum head and sweep to the right, pass the "2" or whichever count is marked to the next count, i.e., "let 3."

Left Hand
Tap "an" or "let" count and brush back to the left, pass "4" or whichever count is marked to next count.

A broken line means to lift brush to next beat or count mark in the direction of the arrow.

A dark filled circle means that the beat is tapped (tick or tap sound).

Ride Rhythm in Jazz

The ride rhythm refers to the basic rhythmic figure or pattern played with a stick on the cymbal or with wire brushes on the snare drum for accompanying a soloist or backing up the ensemble.

There has been much controversy over which is the correct figure or pattern for playing a ride rhythm. I'll clarify this by saying that it depends on the style and the interpretation of that style by the musicians playing.

For those of us brought up during the swing and the bebop eras, the altered triplet on the second and fourth beats of the bar is prevalent since the styles and rhythmic interpretation of the music are based on the triplet.

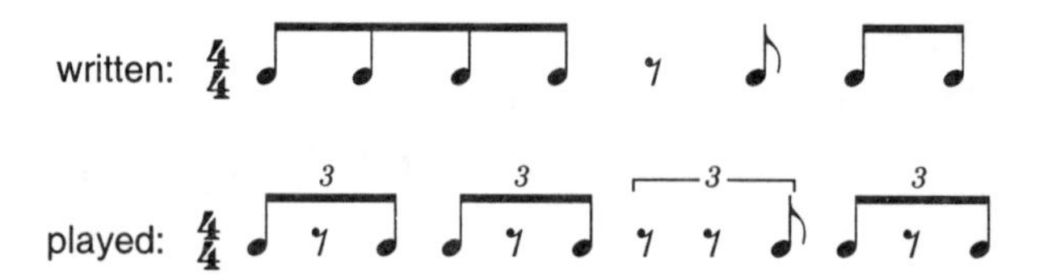

With this interpretation of the rhythm of the melody, the altered triplet used on the second and fourth beats of the ride rhythm fits more naturally.

ride rhythm:

melody:

Many traditional or Dixieland style players make much use of straight eighth or sixteenth notes, that is, their syncopated rhythmic interpretation of the music in this style is based on these dominant mini-pulse beats. For accompaniment at medium to medium-fast tempos in this style, you will find that the standard notated ride rhythm will fit.

This rhythm is also very effective for getting a double-time feeling when playing in a slow ballad tempo, with the left hand still maintaining the full circle or the basic left-hand sweep from left to right to left to right, and so on.

When playing at a very fast tempo, will be the natural ride pattern for swing, Dixieland, bebop, gospel, or country-western styles.

For playing shuffle rhythm, the altered triplet will generally fit in any style.

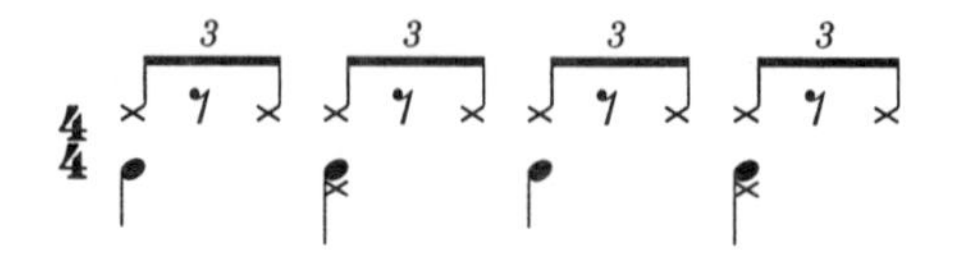

Brush Strokes for Playing Time
(Medium to Fast Tempos)

One must remember that when it is the drummer's primary function to establish a steady, smooth, swinging pulse for the other instrumentalist to build on, simplicity is the key.

The basic left-hand time brush sweep is shown in the diagram below on this page.

I suggest you trace this and all of the other diagrams laid out in this book with your bare hand first, allowing yourself to get the feeling of each stroke in your fingertips. Next go over the area with your brush in tempo, smooth and lightly.

The dark area represents the stroke area to be covered by the left-hand brush when playing the "shhh" sound or sweep. The idea is to think of a smooth rhythmic movement, somewhat like a pendulum in constant motion. To aid you, I have placed ground pulse beat numerals and mini-pulse count syllables at the approximate areas the brush should be passing or striking, whichever the case may be.

Execution

Starting from the left-hand side of the drum with the left hand, tap the first beat of the first bar or measure and continue in a sweeping motion from left to right and back again right to left in a continuous movement in tempo. One way to get the feeling of smoothness is to count slowly in an even mini-pulse, for example, 1 an 2 an 3 an 4 an 1 trip-let 2 trip-let 3 trip-let 4 trip-let or 1 e an ah 2 e an ah 3 e an ah 4 e an ah. I would like to re-emphasize the importance of the brush passing the numbered or syllable stroke areas in sync with the verbal count. This procedure will allow the feel of the G.P. to change while still maintaining a steady tempo.

Basic Left-Hand Time Stroke (Sounds = "Shhhhhs—shhhhh—shhhhh—shhhhh")

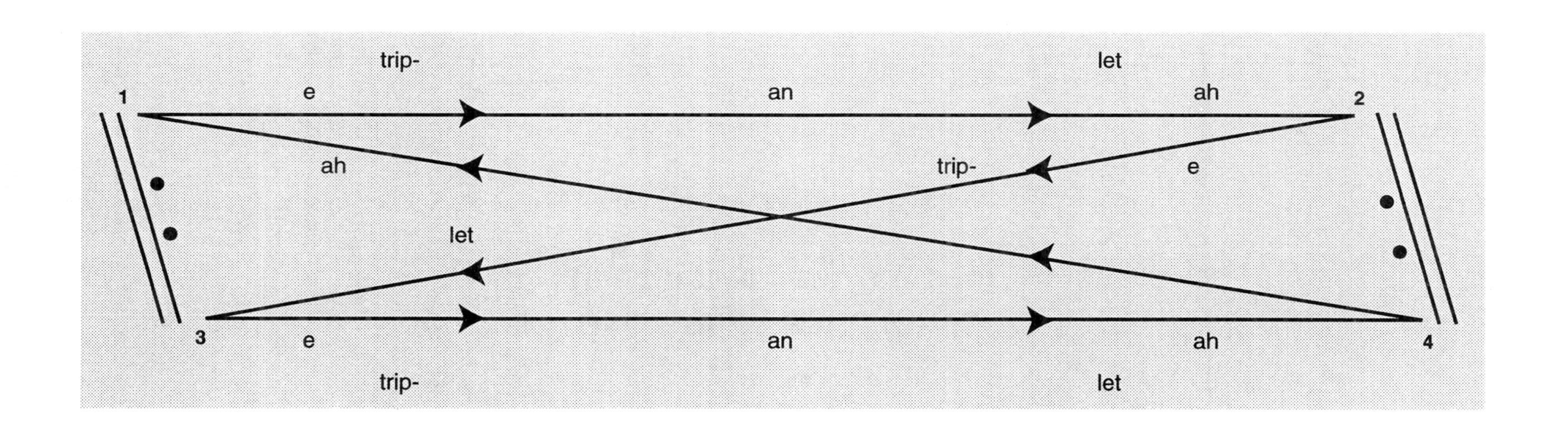

Basic Right-Hand Stroke
(Medium to Fast Tempos)

This stroke or beat is based on the same rhythmic pattern as the basic ride cymbal pattern.

The right-hand stroke or beat starts on the right-hand side of the drum with a “tick” of the first beat, count “1.” Lift the brush and tap the “2” count with a slight accent to the left-hand side of the drum head. You then count or say the syllable “trip-” as you lift the brush from the “2” count, over to the right and tick the “let-3” counts in the right-hand area as shown in the diagram. The count “4” is tapped with a little accent in the same area as the “2” count (to the left). Next, count “trip-” as you lift the brush and move to tick the “let-1” counts in the area to the right. The last “one” count is the start of the next measure or bar, which is repeated in the same manner.

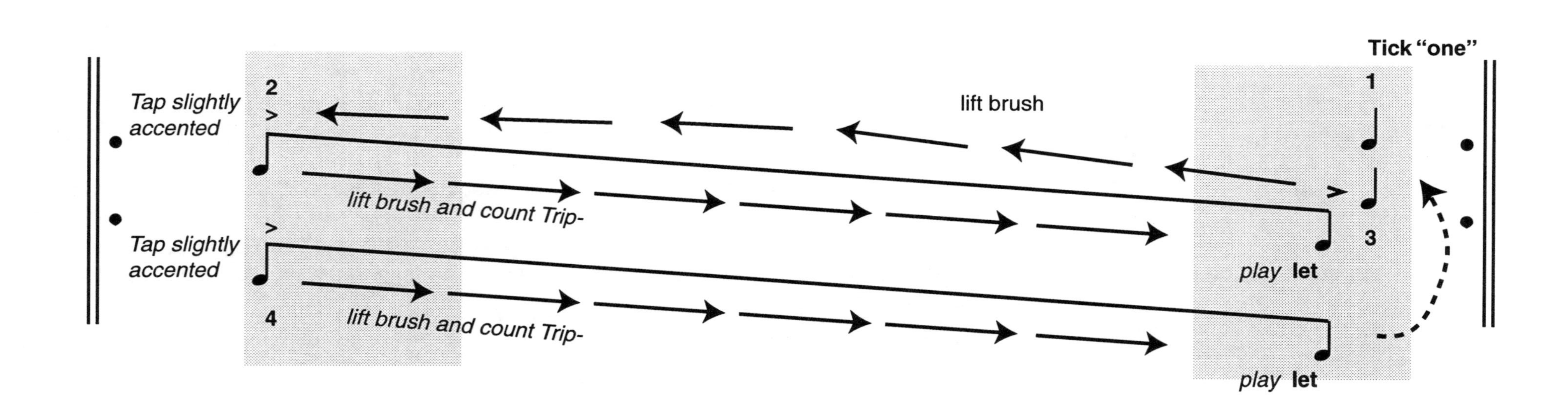

Combined Basic Right- and Left-Hand Time Strokes
(Medium to Fast Tempos)

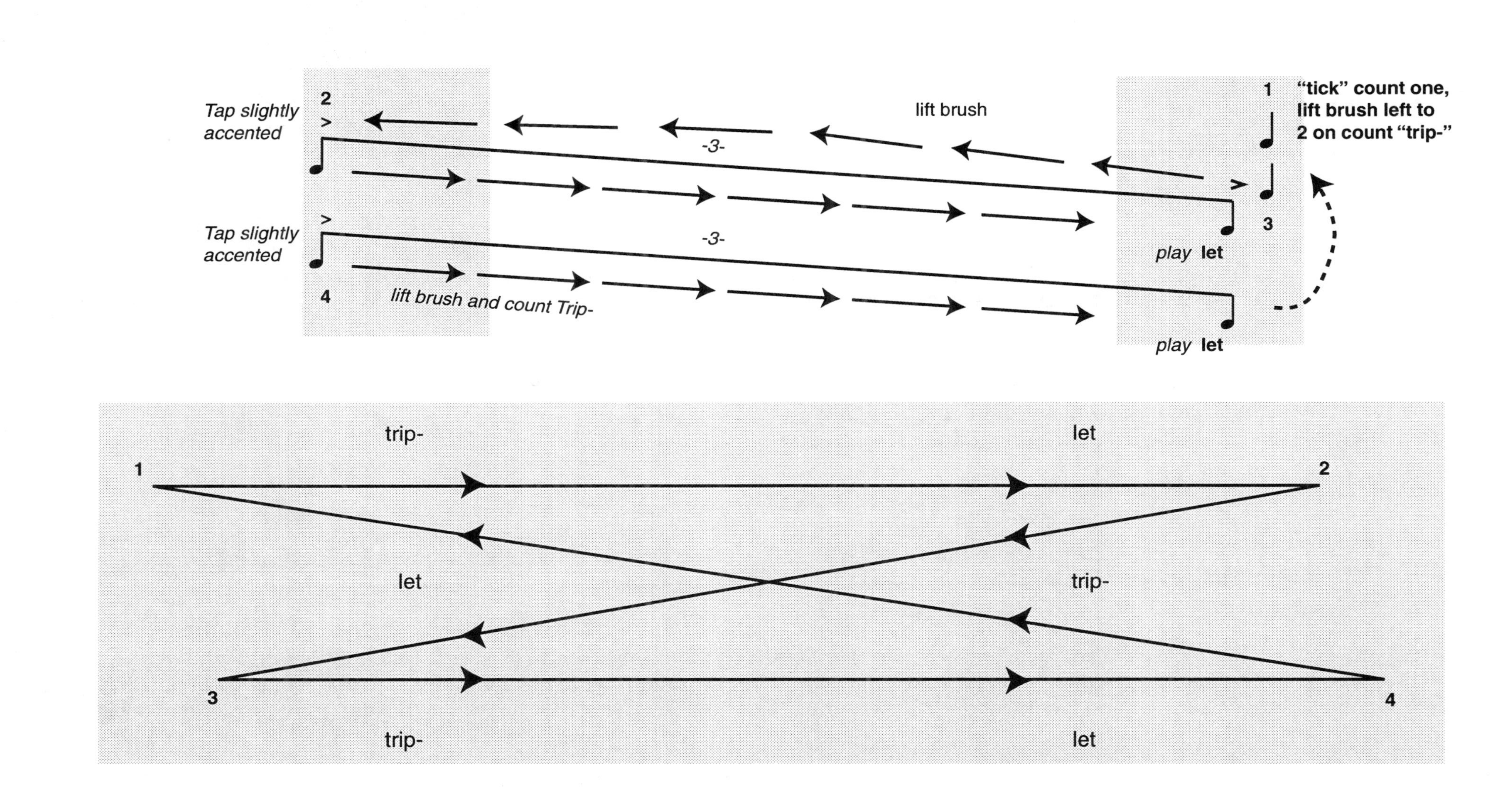

Phrasing in Time (Tempo)

When playing in a jazz 4/4 or 2 feeling, you will notice that most standard, show, swing, bebop, blues, gospel, and country-western tunes are written in combinations of two-, four-, or eight-bar phrases. It will be valuable to learn to punctuate these groups of phrases while still keeping time (the tempo) swinging and steady. This can be done as follows:

You will notice that in the last bar of each of the phrases, the third and fourth beats are altered. On the third beat, the "let" count is tied to the down-beat of 4 and proceeds with the "let" of "4 trip-" to the "one" count of the next phrase.

The diagrams on the following pages show how this stroke is played on the drum.

Right-Hand Punctuation

Remember that the diagram shows only the approximate area the stroke can cover. The total area of the head from right to left can be used, or when playing at a faster tempo the distance between beats may be shorter. In either case, keep the pulse count even.

The last bar of the phrase

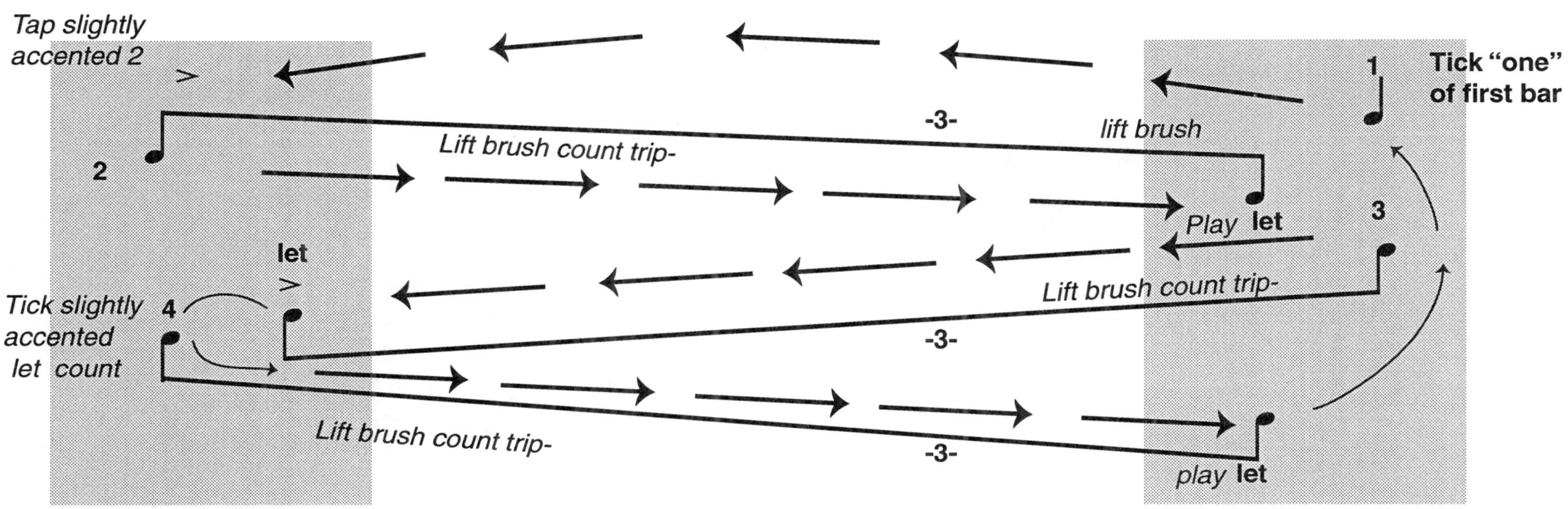

Tap slightly accented 2

\>

2

Lift brush count trip-

-3-

lift brush

1

Tick "one" of first bar

Play **let**

3

Lift brush count trip-

-3-

let

\>

Tick slightly accented let count 4

Lift brush count trip-

-3-

play **let**

The Substitute "An" Count

In very fast tempos, the count of "an-4-an-1" should be substituted for the "-let 4 triplet 1" because the figure automatically becomes eighth notes when played fast. This will also apply when making the punctuation with the left hand, for example, 1 an 2 an 3 an 4 an.

Right-Hand Punctuation With Basic Left-Hand Brush Stroke

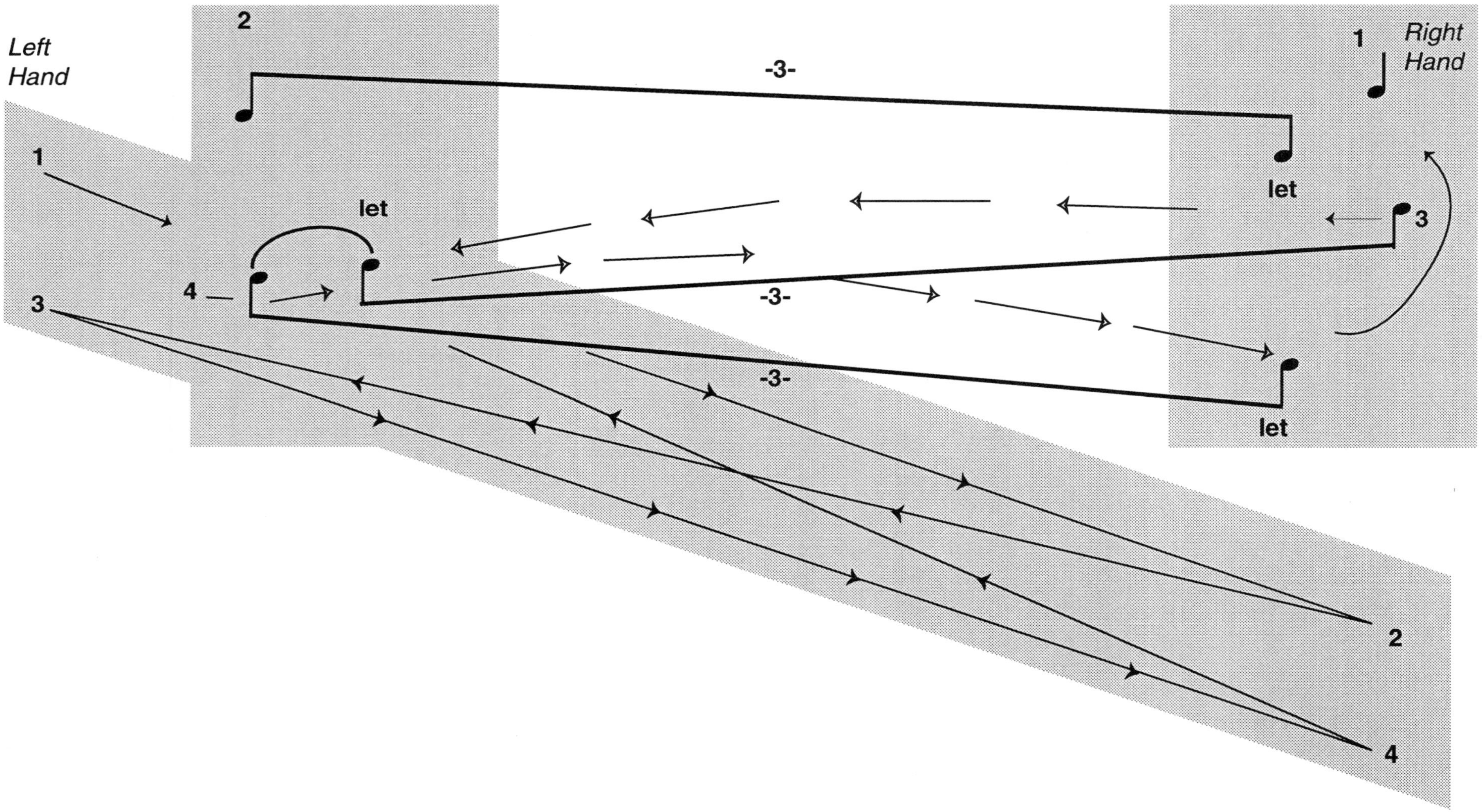

Left-Hand Punctuation

For making the punctuation with the left hand, the figure will look like this on the drum:
Count in triplets: 1 trip - let 2 trip - let 3 trip - let 4 trip - let

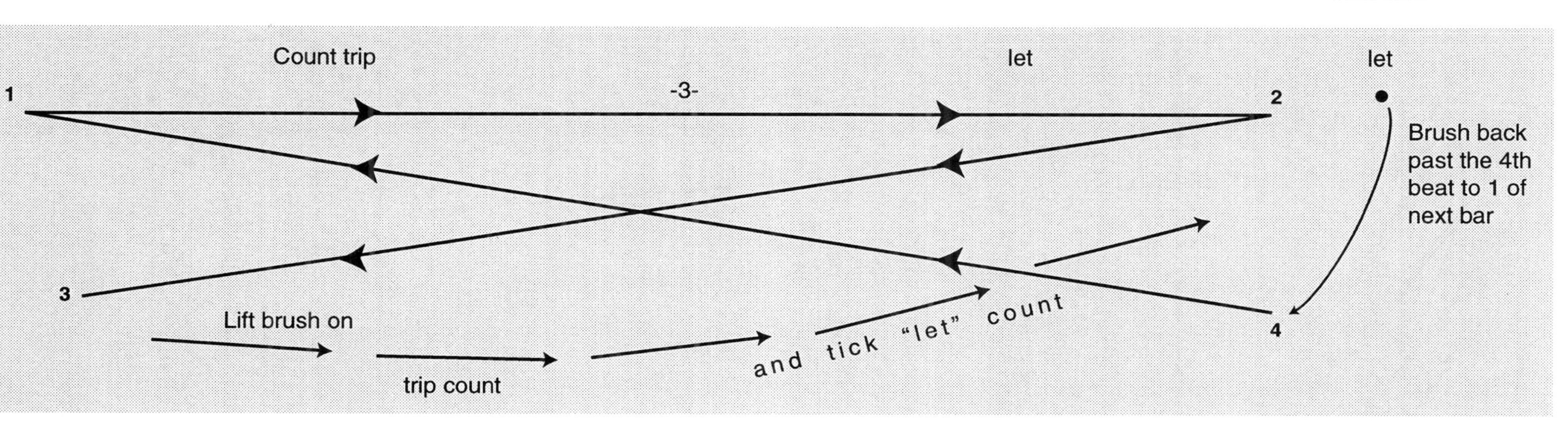

Note: Remember to lift the brush to the right on the counts of "3 trip-" over to the right side of the 4. Leave the brush on the drum head and sweep back past the 4th count or beat in tempo (time) to the "one" of the next measure.

Left-Hand Punctuation With Right-Hand Ride Pattern

Note: The combination of the left-hand punctuation with the basic right-hand ride pattern can give an accented "an 4" or "let 4" ending to each phrase. It can also create a lead-in or pick-up to the next phrase if you play the "let" count of the fourth beat distinctly.

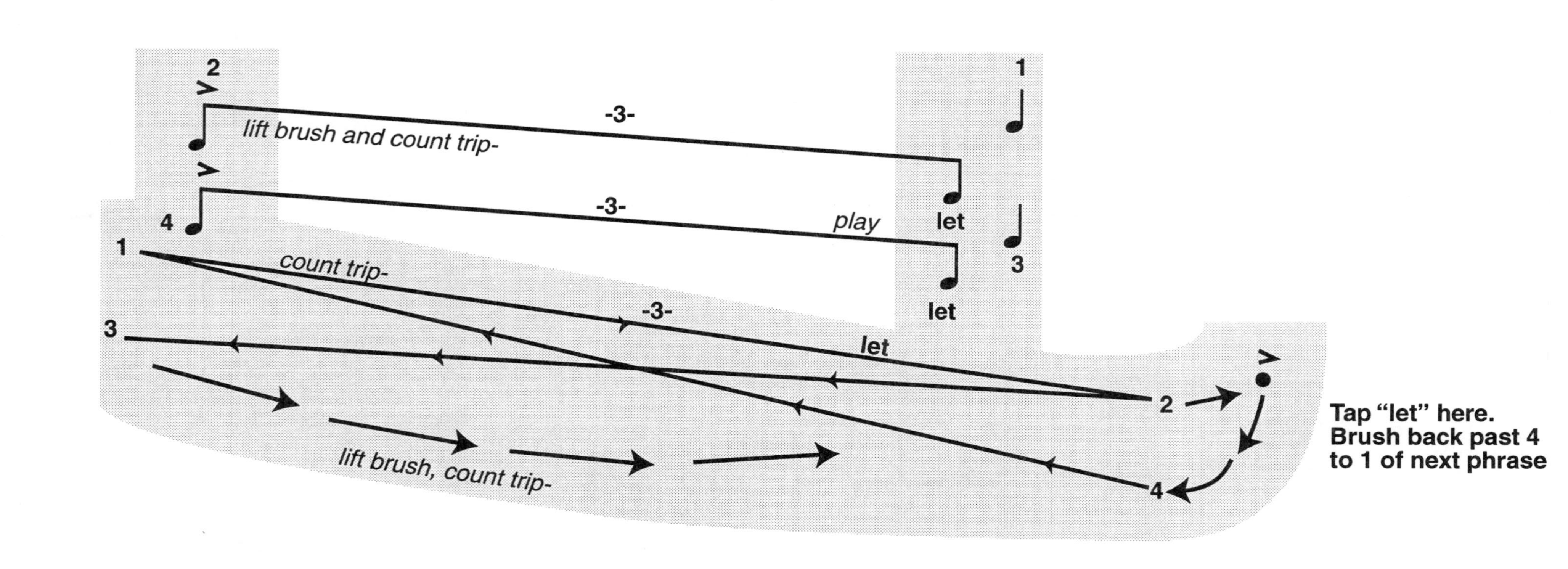

Accented Right Hand on "Let" Count of First G.P. Beat (Playing Right-Hand "Ride Rhythm")

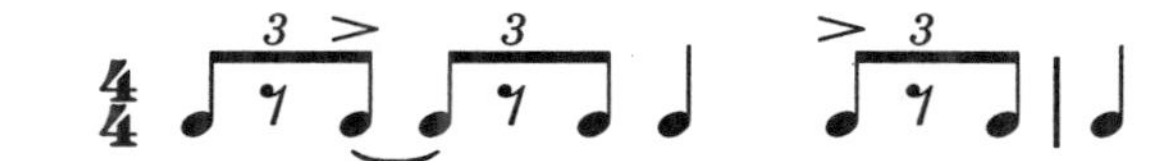

Tap Accented "let"

Right Hand

1 count trip- lift brush

let >

-3-

2 lift brush count trip- -3- play -let

3

4 lift brush count trip- -3- play -let

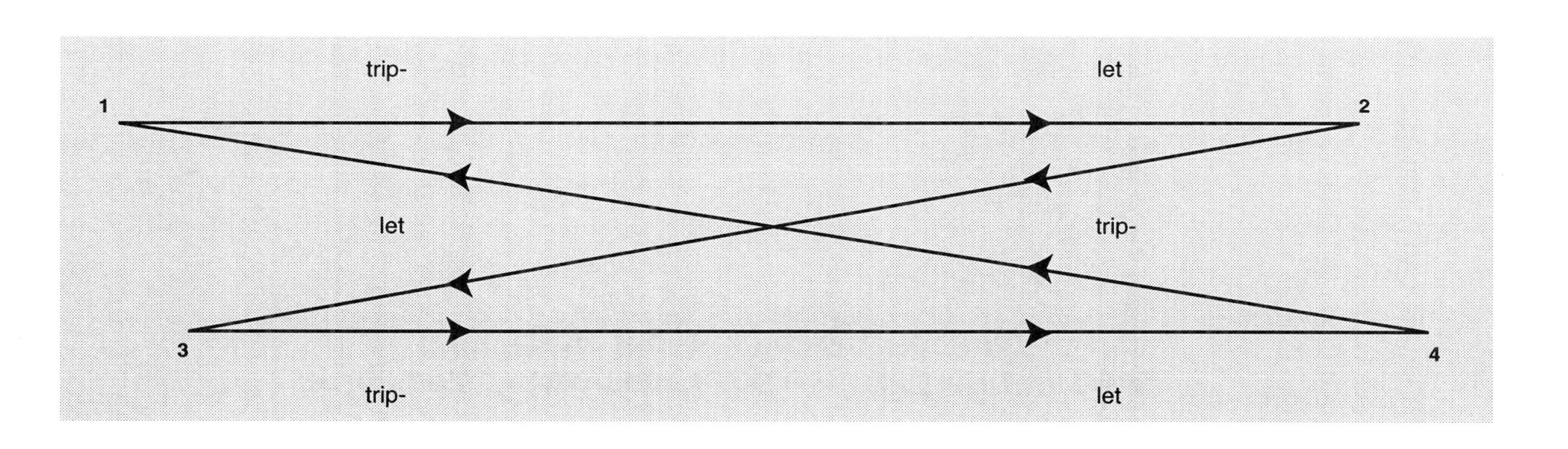

Accented Left Hand on "Let Count" of First G.P. Beat (With Basic Right-Hand Ride Rhythm)

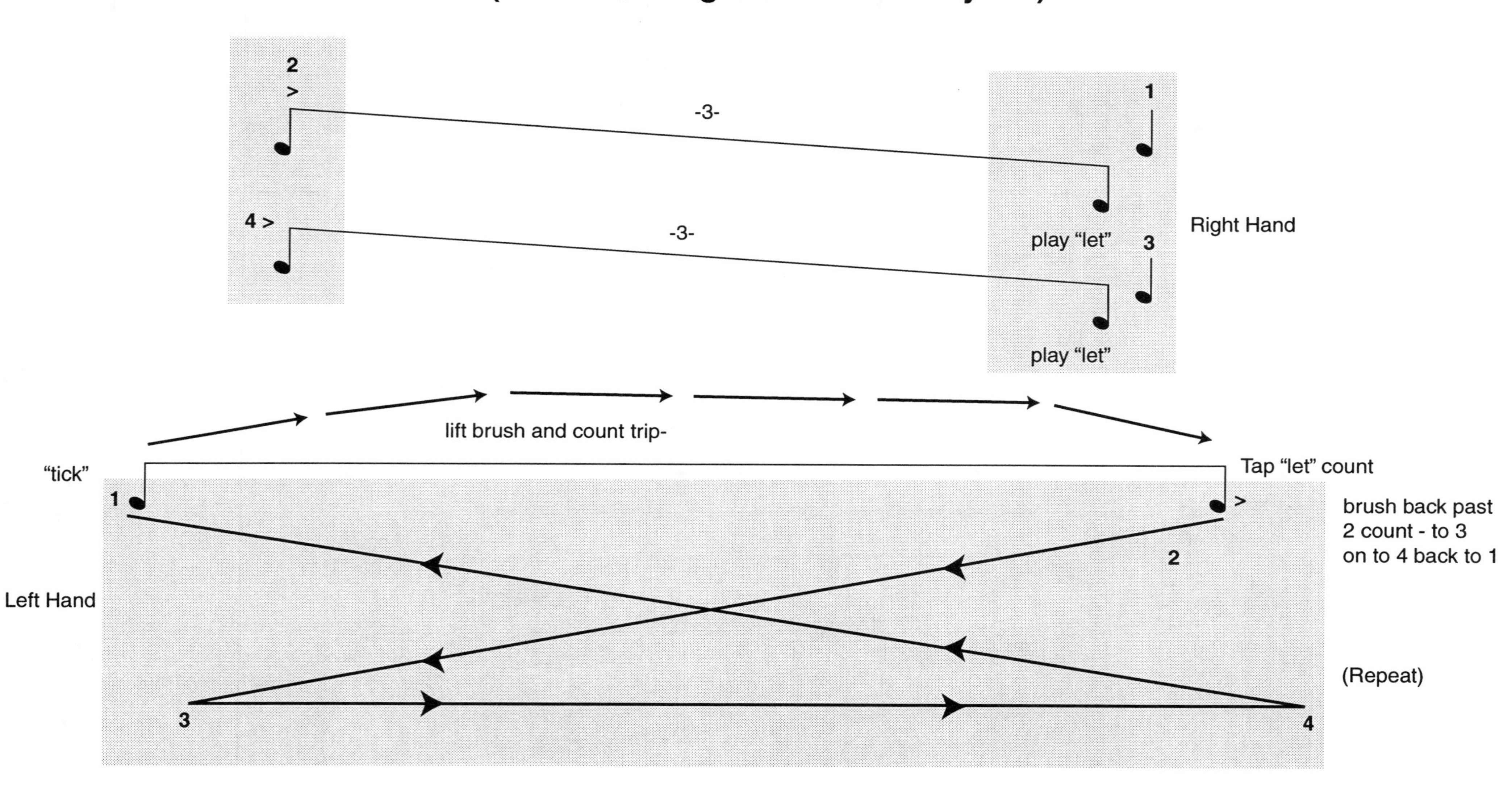

Remember to activate desired mini-pulse count/feel

Accented "Let" Count of Second G.P. Beat (Playing Right-Hand Ride Rhythm)

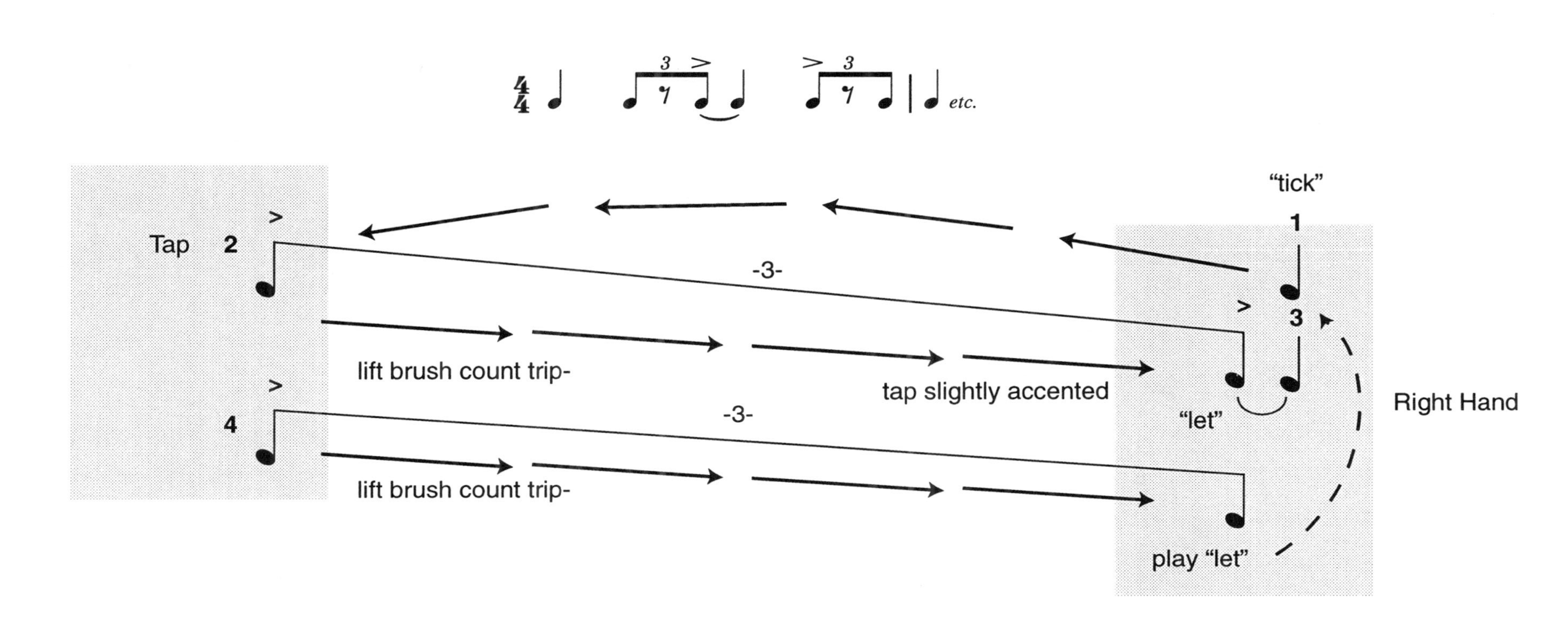

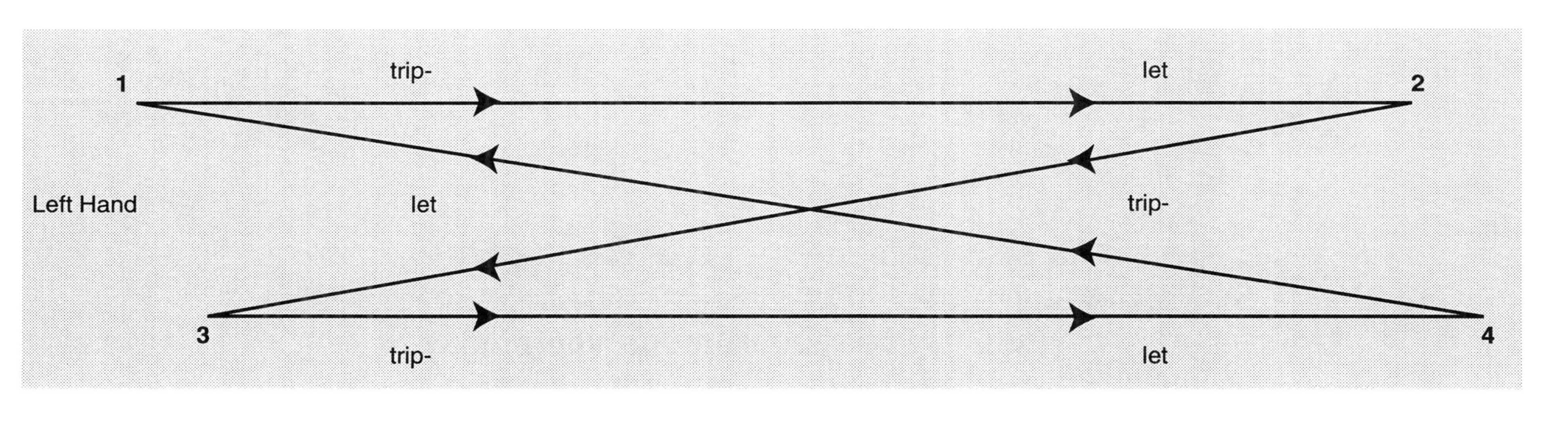

Accented Left Hand on “Let” Count of Second G.P. Beat
(With Basic Right-Hand Ride Rhythm)

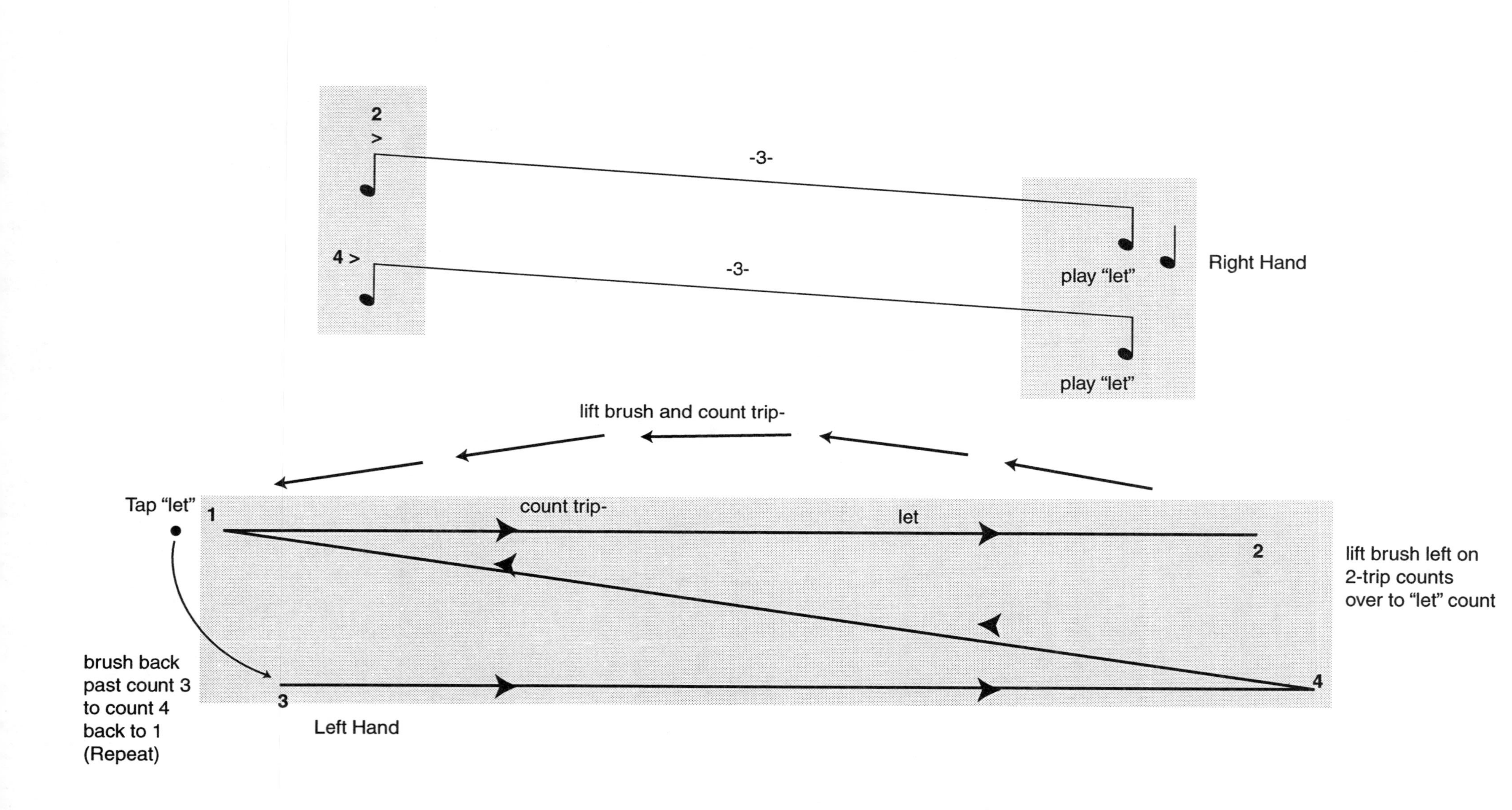

Accented "Let" Count of Fourth G.P. Beat
(Playing Right-Hand Ride Rhythm)

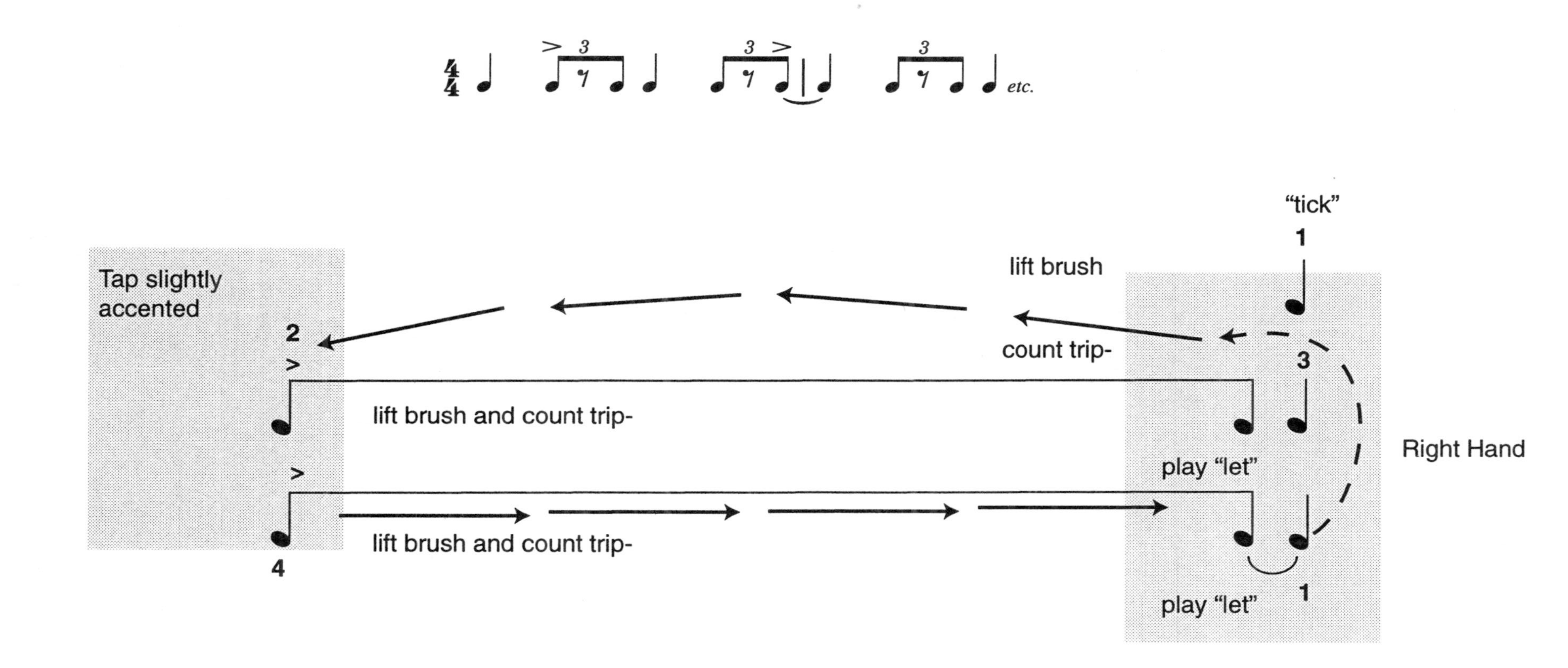

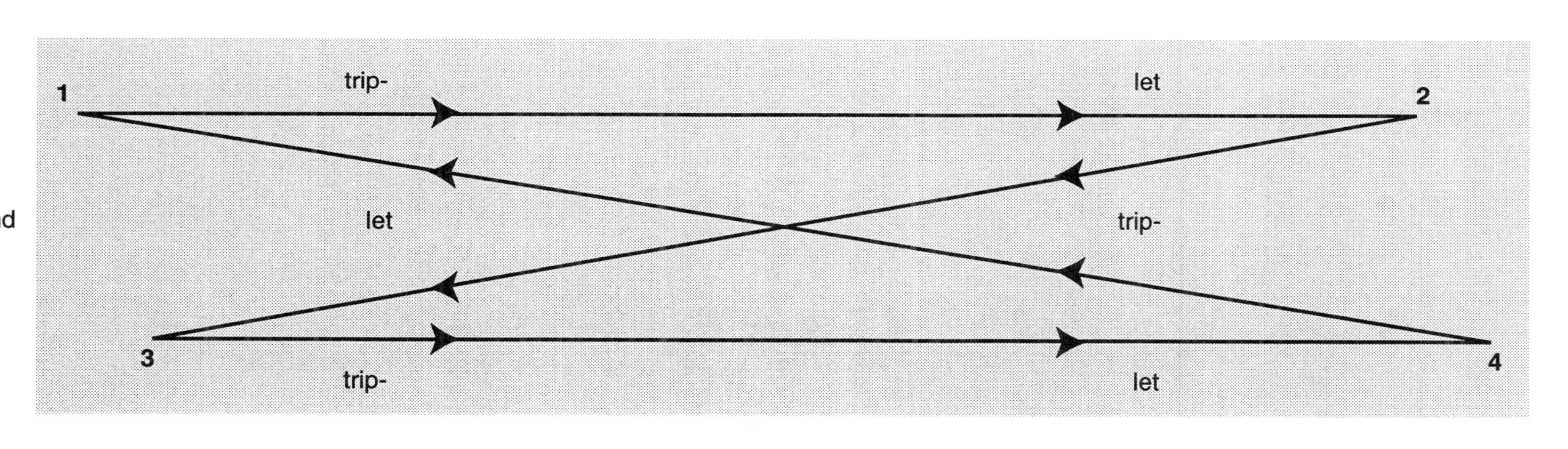

Accented Left Hand on "Let" Count of Fourth G.P. Beat (With Basic Right-Hand Ride Rhythm)

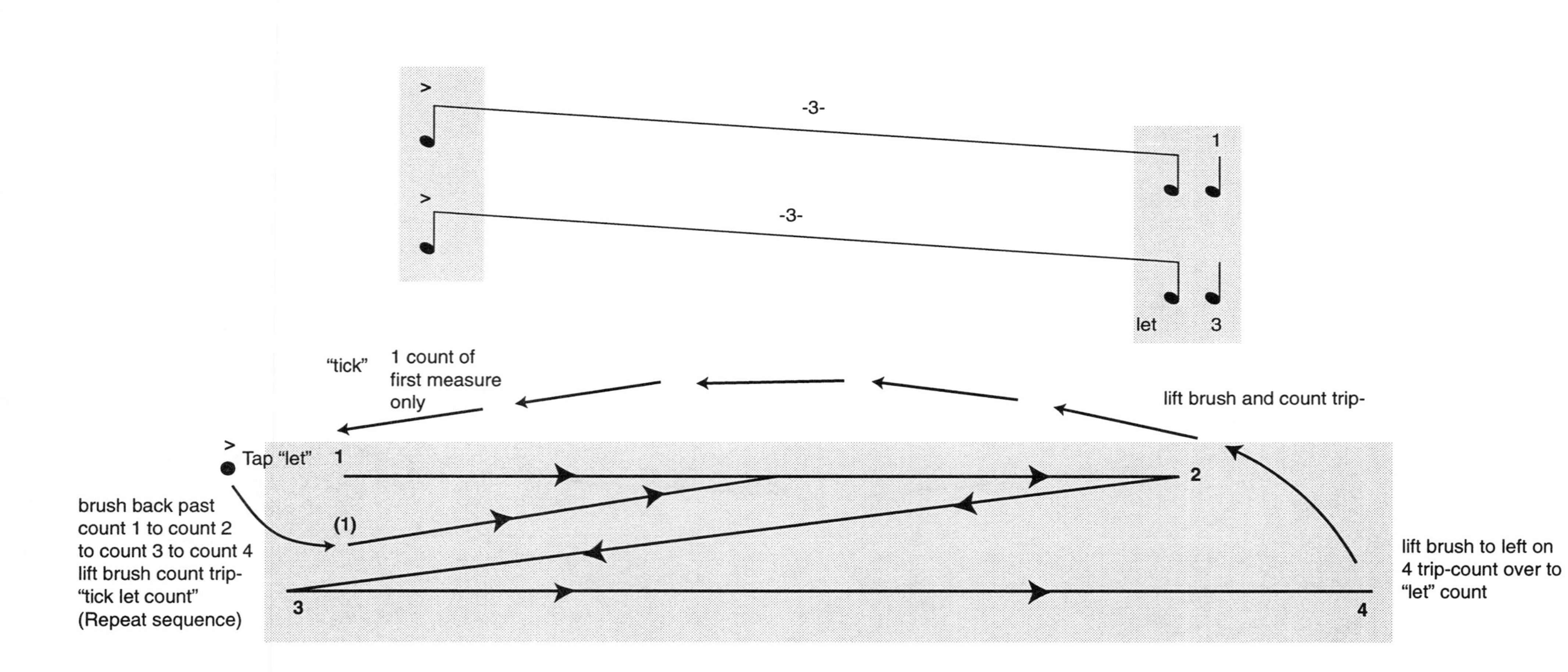

Basic Left-Hand Sweep With Right-Hand Tap (Tick Sound)

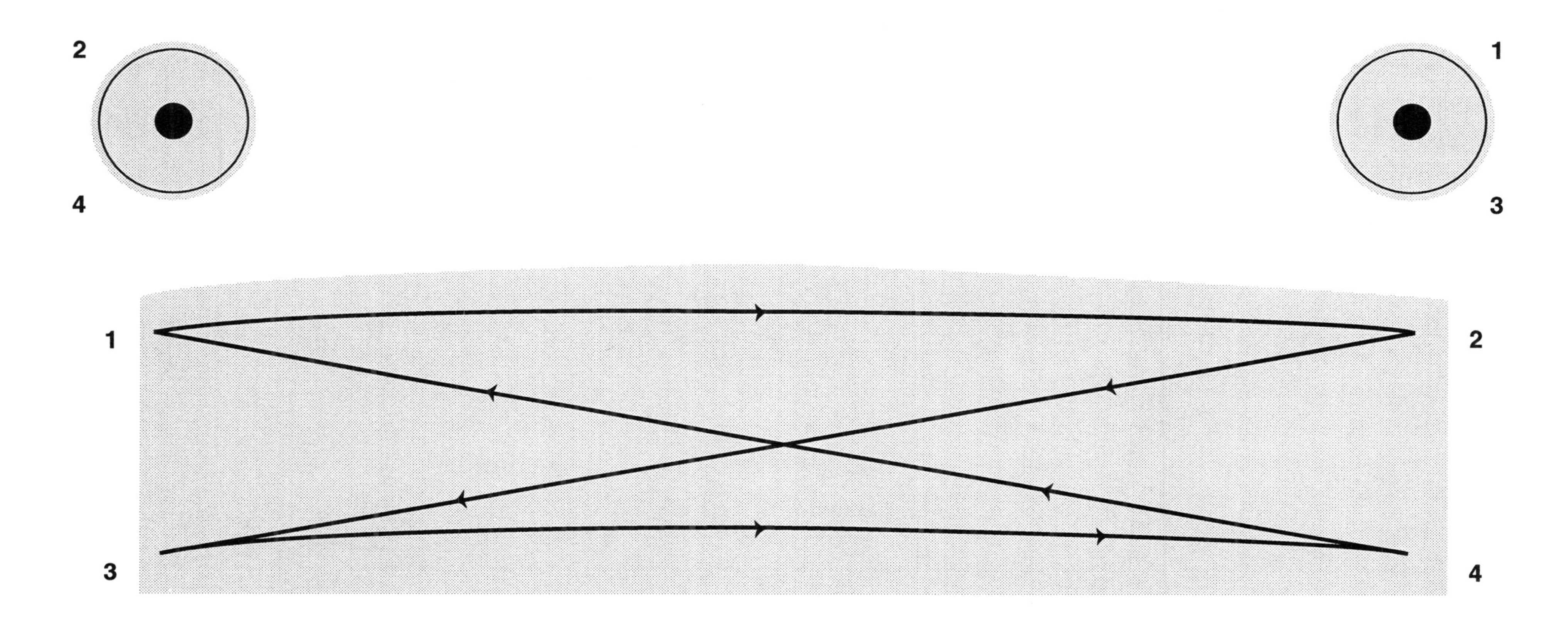

Note: This stroke is very effective for a light, steady 4/4 pulse.

Left-Hand Half Circle

This stroke can be used as an alternative to the full circle.

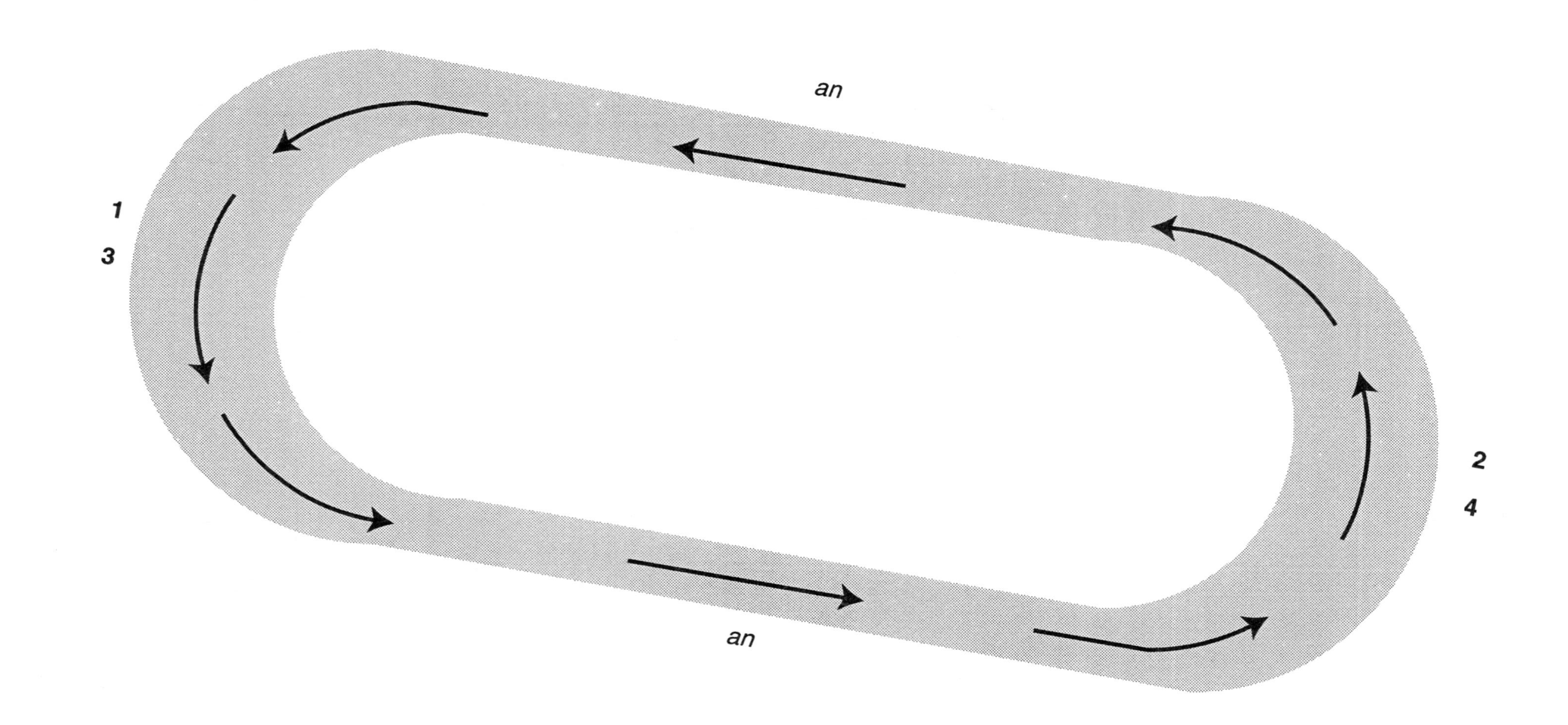

Left-Hand Full-Circle Stroke

This stroke is basically for slow tempos but can be used effectively at medium tempos.

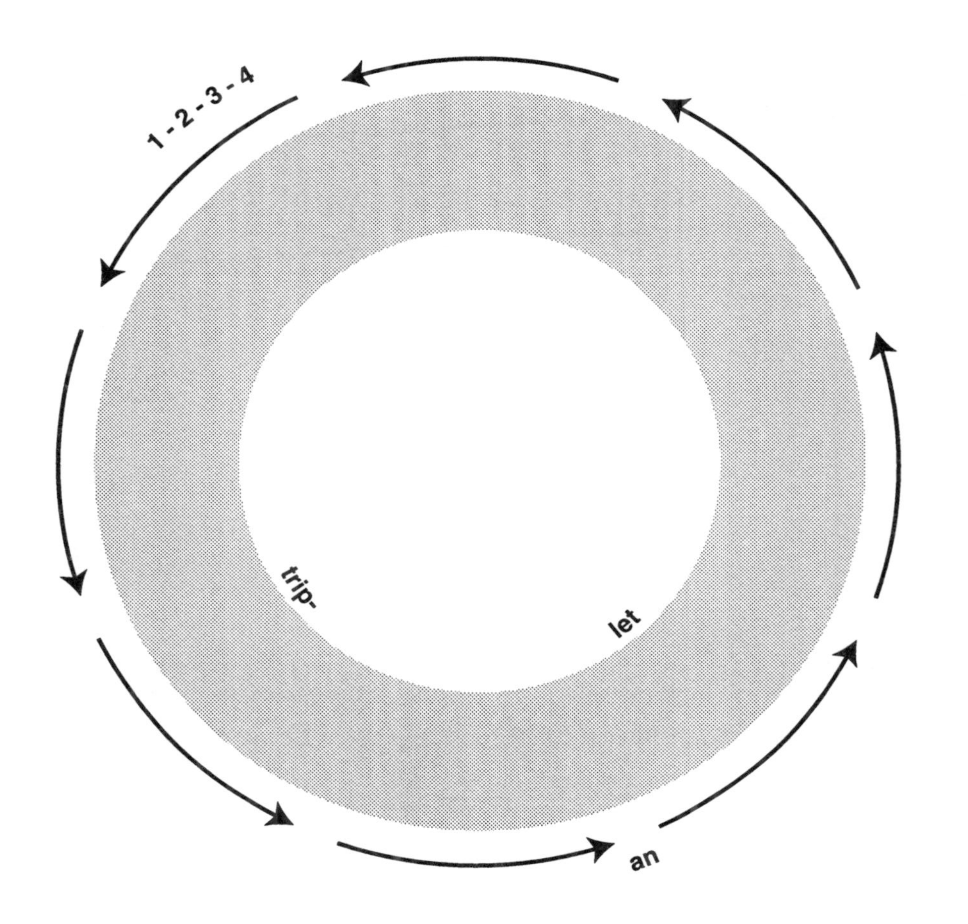

The numbers and syllables show the approximate areas the hand should be passing when using either the eighth note (1 an 2 an, etc.) or triplet count.

Although many players play this stroke moving in a clockwise motion, I use a counterclockwise movement for balance between the hands when the right-hand strokes are combined with the full circle of the left hand.

Right-Hand Hook Stroke

For the right-hand hook stroke, start again with the hand tracing the diagram, adding the brush after you have the feeling of the stroke in your fingertips.

While you are practicing this stroke, I would like to point out how your imagination might aid you in getting a particular feeling in your playing.

The sound I want from you is soft, smooth, almost airy. Think of someone or some pet you love. Now try to imagine how you might brush or stroke his or her hair or its fur or feathers. Try it again.

Other points to remember in this stroke are the striking of the first beat of the first bar, the lightly accented second and fourth beats of every bar, and the lifts from the first to second beat and third to fourth beats, and so on.

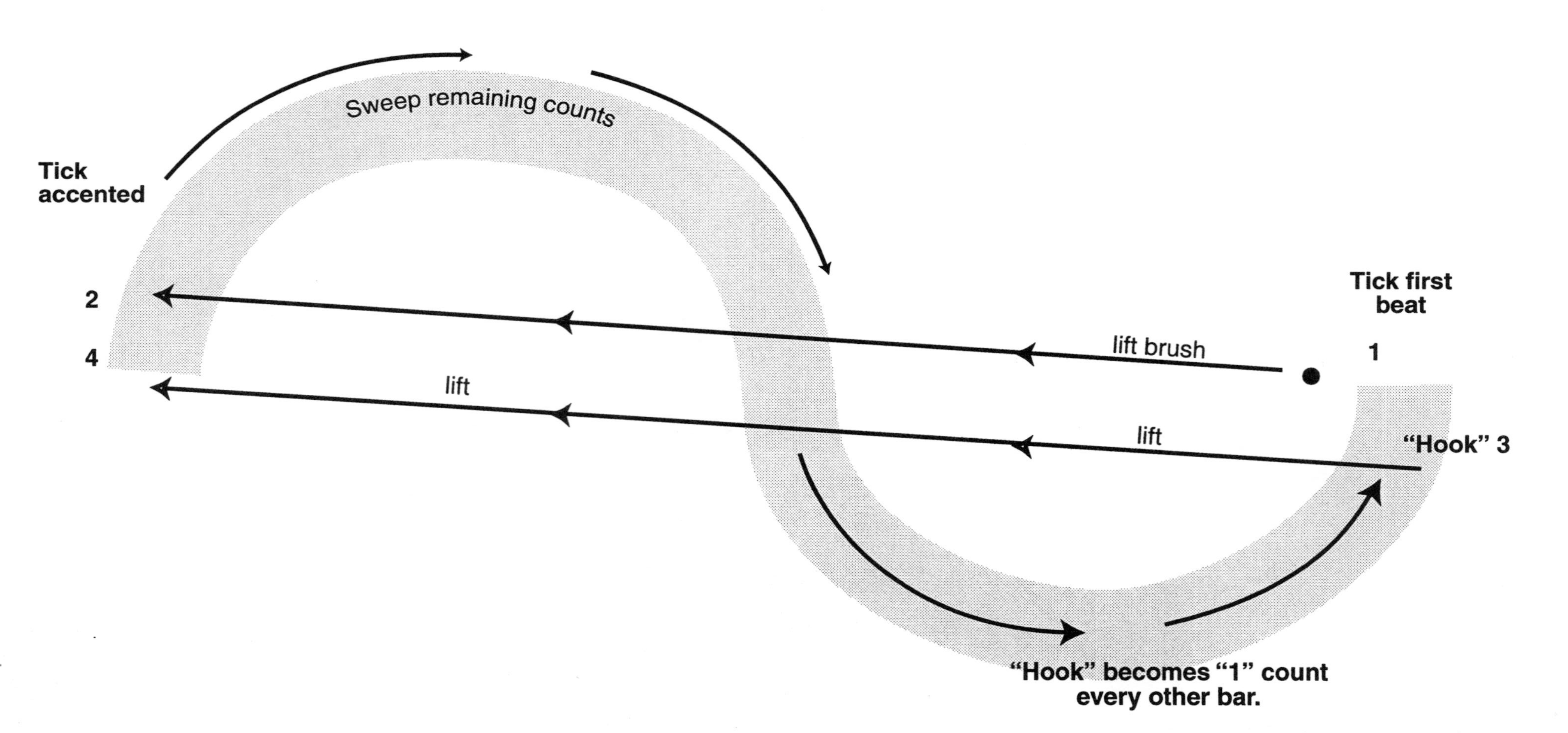

Right-Hand Hook Stroke
(With Left-Hand Half Circle)

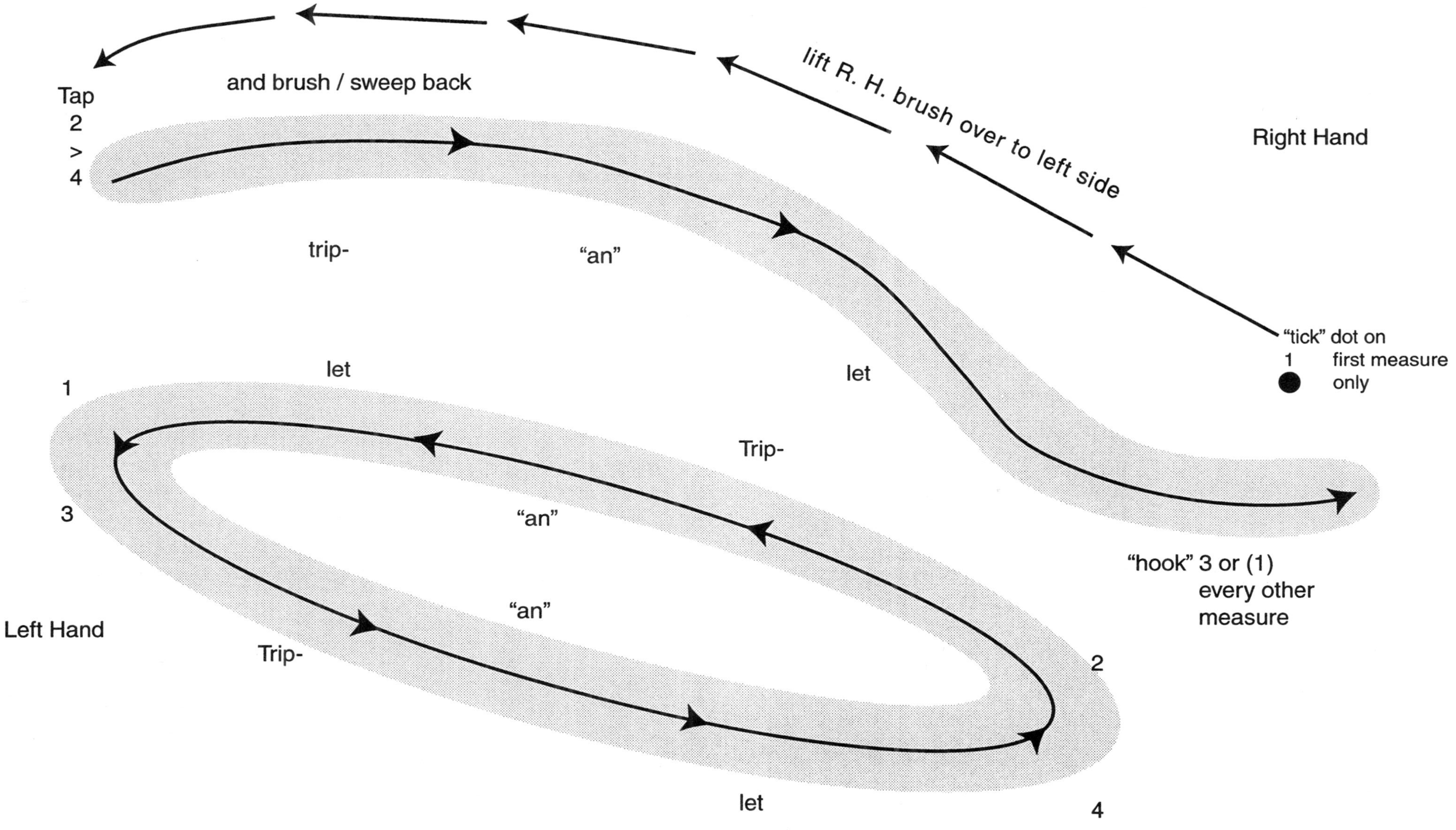

Right Hand

lift R. H. brush over to left side

and brush / sweep back

Tap
2
>
4

trip-

"an"

let

"tick" dot on
1 first measure
only

"hook" 3 or (1)
every other
measure

1

let

Trip-

"an"

3

"an"

Left Hand

Trip-

let

2

4

Combination Left-Hand Full Circle and Right-Hand Hook Stroke (Slow Ballad to Medium Tempos)

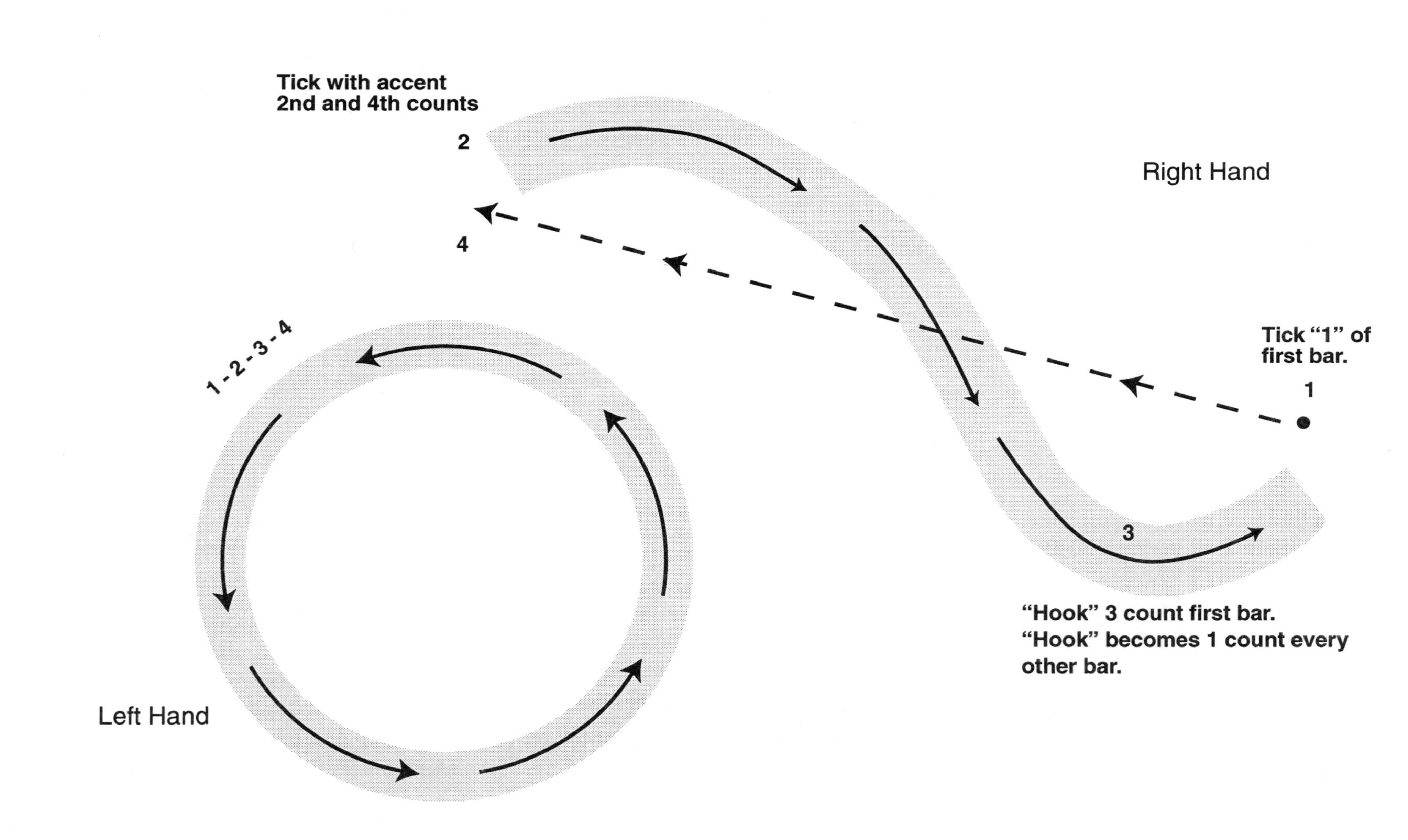

Right-Hand "Zorro" Stroke

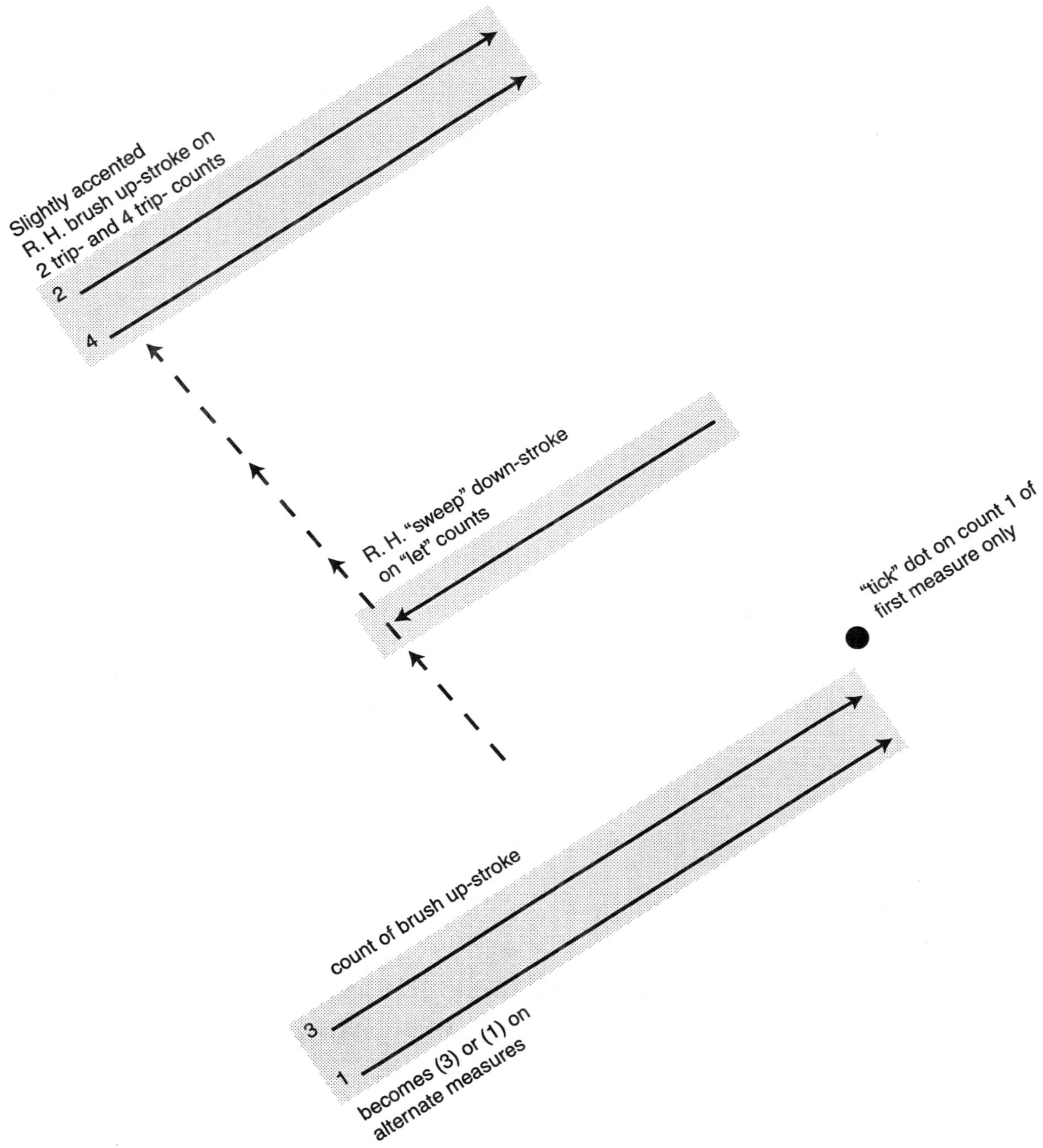

Right-Hand "Zorro" Stroke
(With Left-Hand Half Circle)

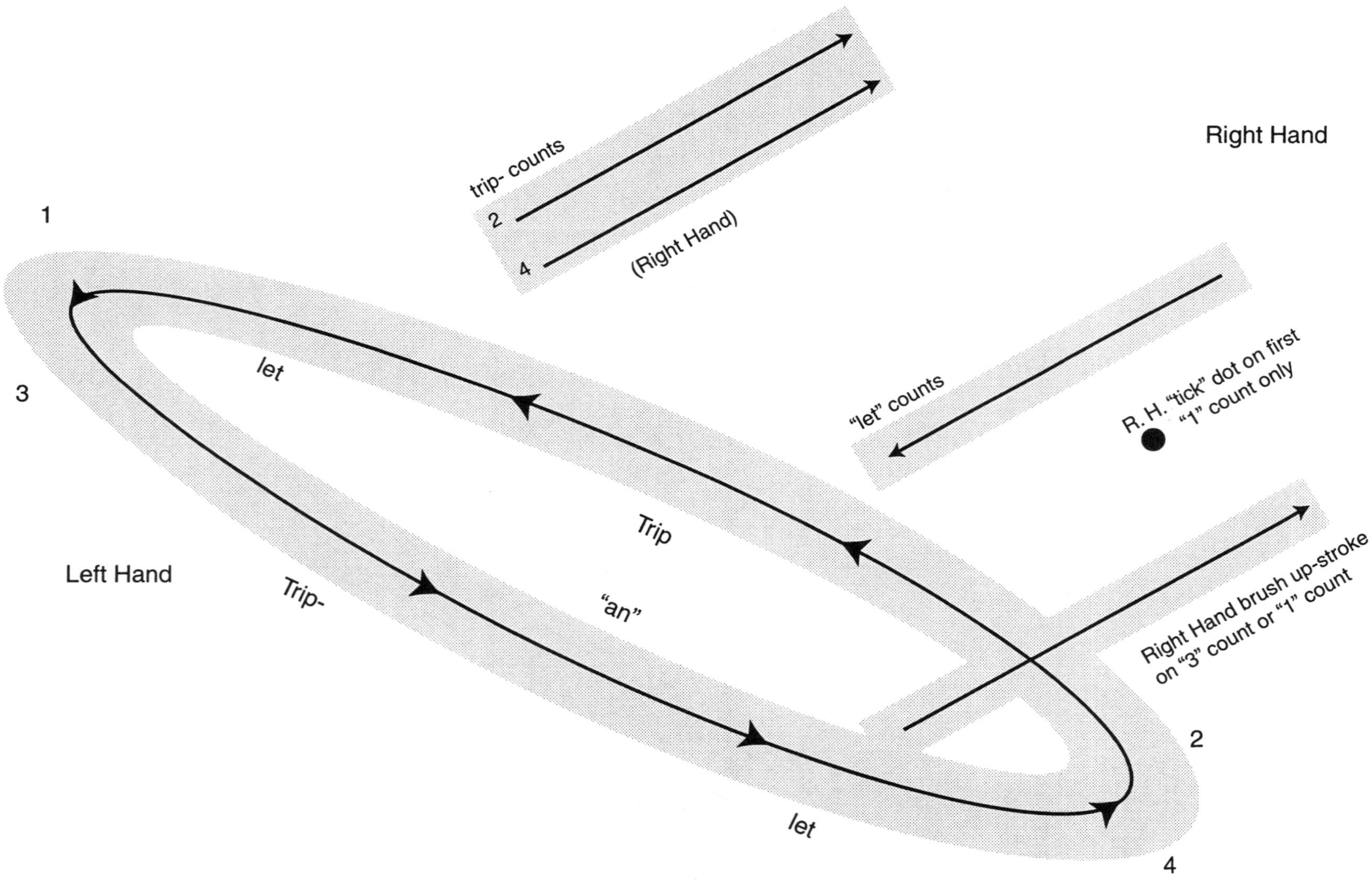

trip- counts
2
4
(Right Hand)

Right Hand

1

3

let

"let" counts

R. H. "tick" dot on first
"1" count only

Trip

Left Hand

Trip-

"an"

Right Hand brush up-stroke
on "3" count or "1" count

2

let

4

Combination Right-Hand "Zorro" Stroke and Left-Hand Full Circle (Medium to Fast Tempos)

Tap and brush right up-stroke on two trip- counts. Repeat on "4 trip-"

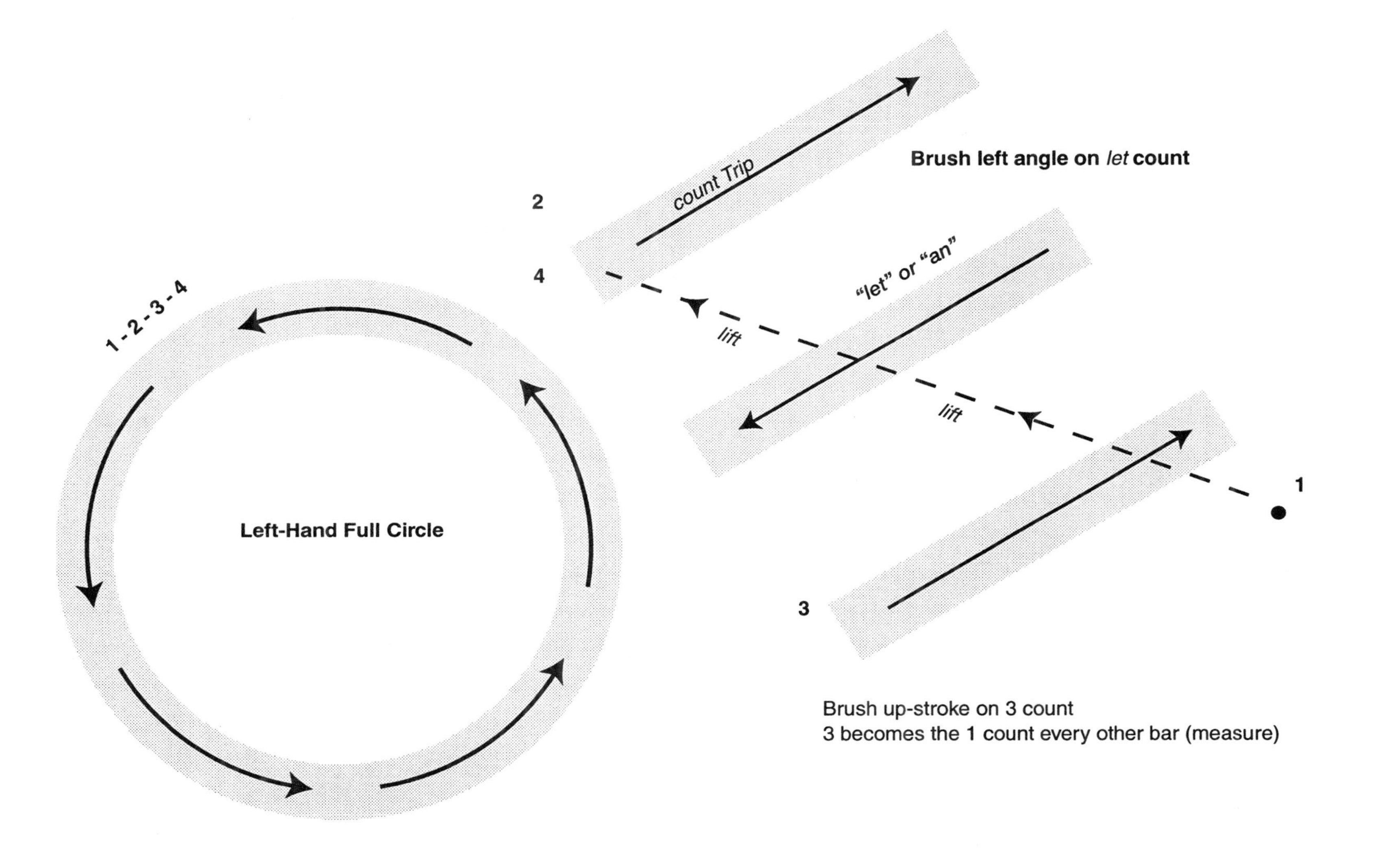

Brush up-stroke on 3 count
3 becomes the 1 count every other bar (measure)

Full Circles (counter motion)

Both hands make circle in counter motion.

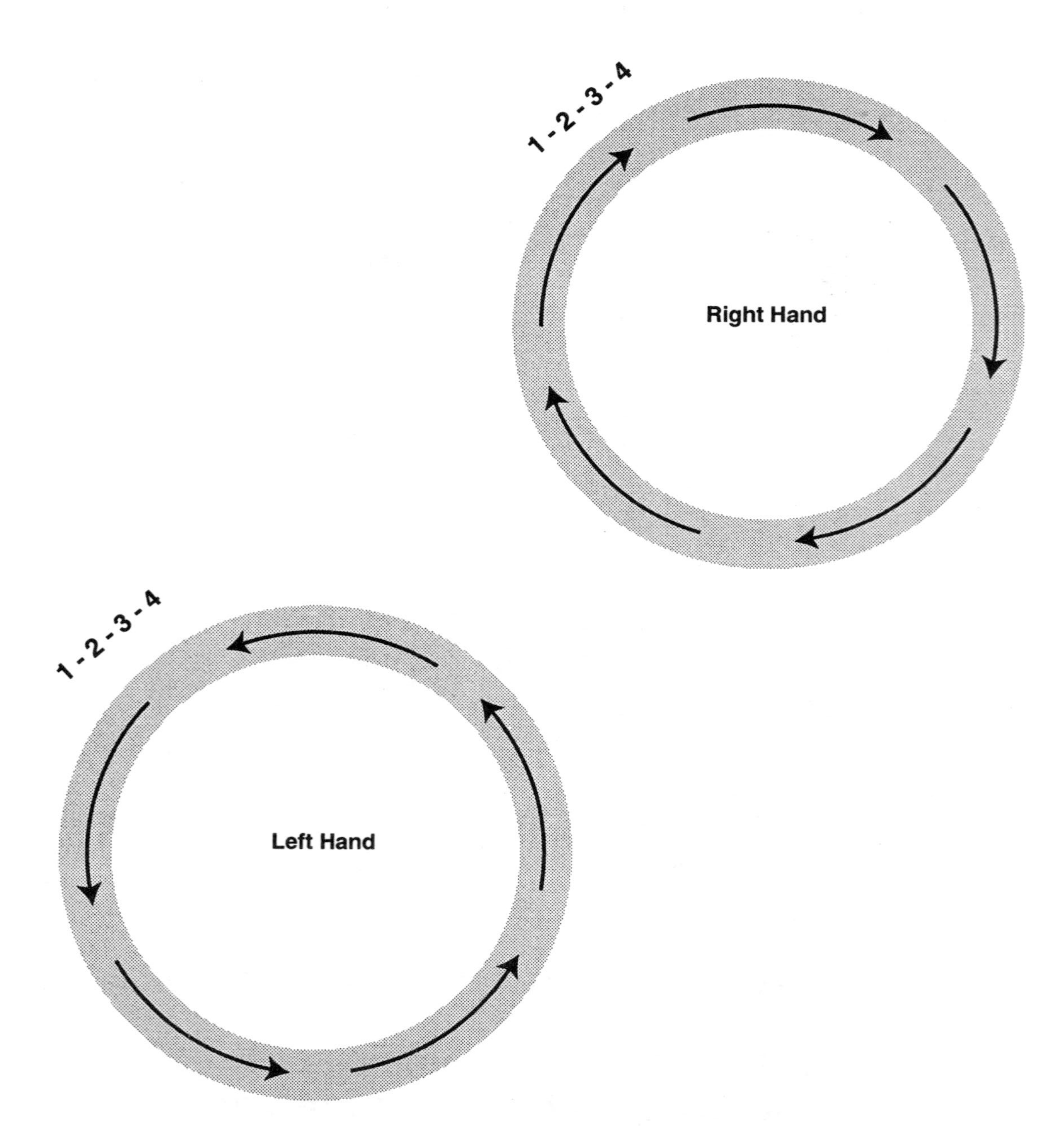

Note: One can also accent in the circle on the “2” and “4” counts by adding a little pressure and slightly accelerating the movement on these counts.

Basic Ride Rhythm in 3/4 Time
(Right- and Left-Hand Strokes)

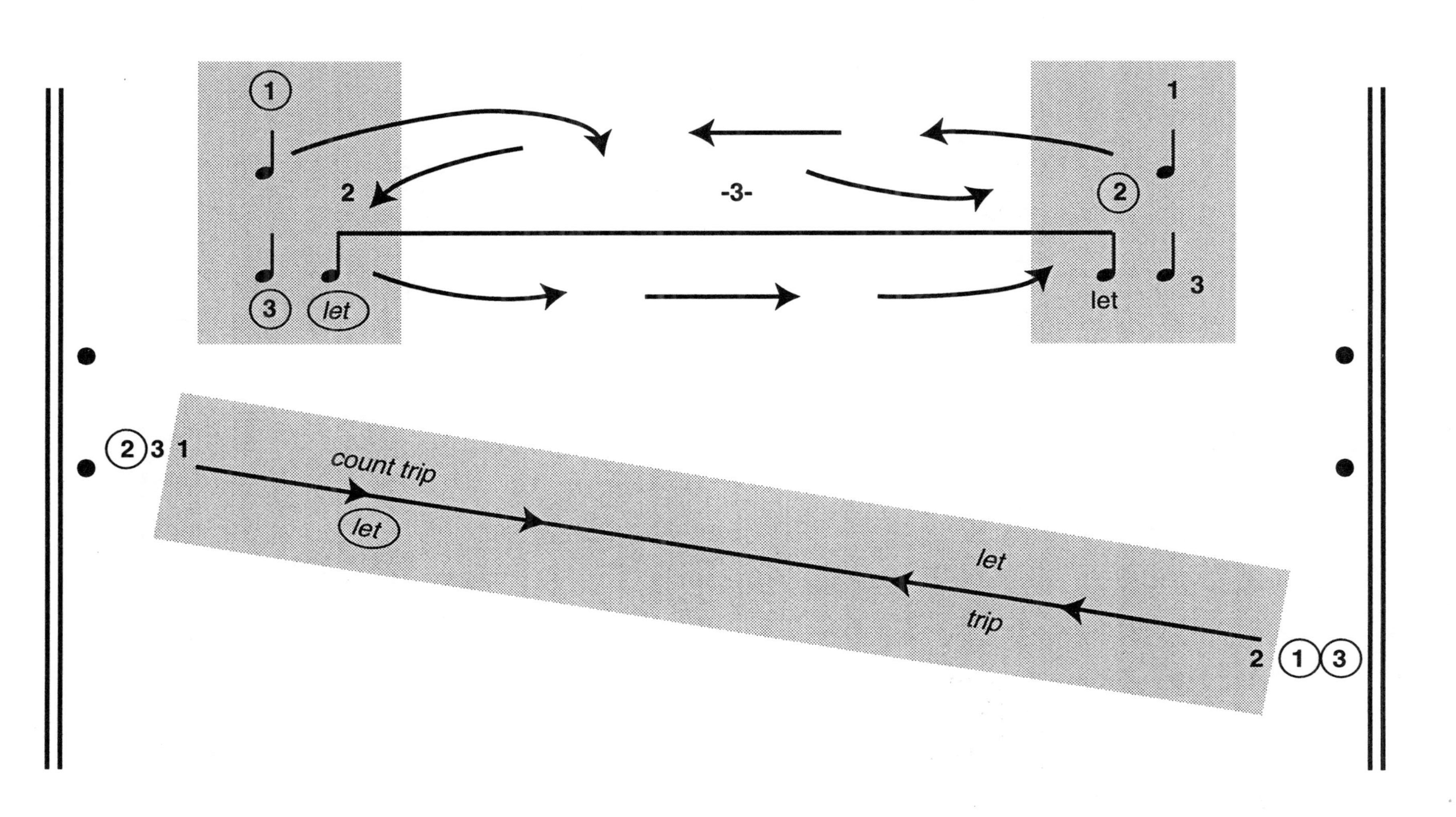

Circled numbers and syllables indicate points of stroke on alternate bars: second, fourth bars, and so on. As you can see, in 3/4 time the position of the hands is reversed every second measure (bar).

Practice each hand separately first, count slowly, and concentrate on getting an even flow to the rhythm. Finally, play both hands together. Circled numbers represent alternate measures.

Accented "Let" Count of First Beat in 3/4 Time (Right Hand)

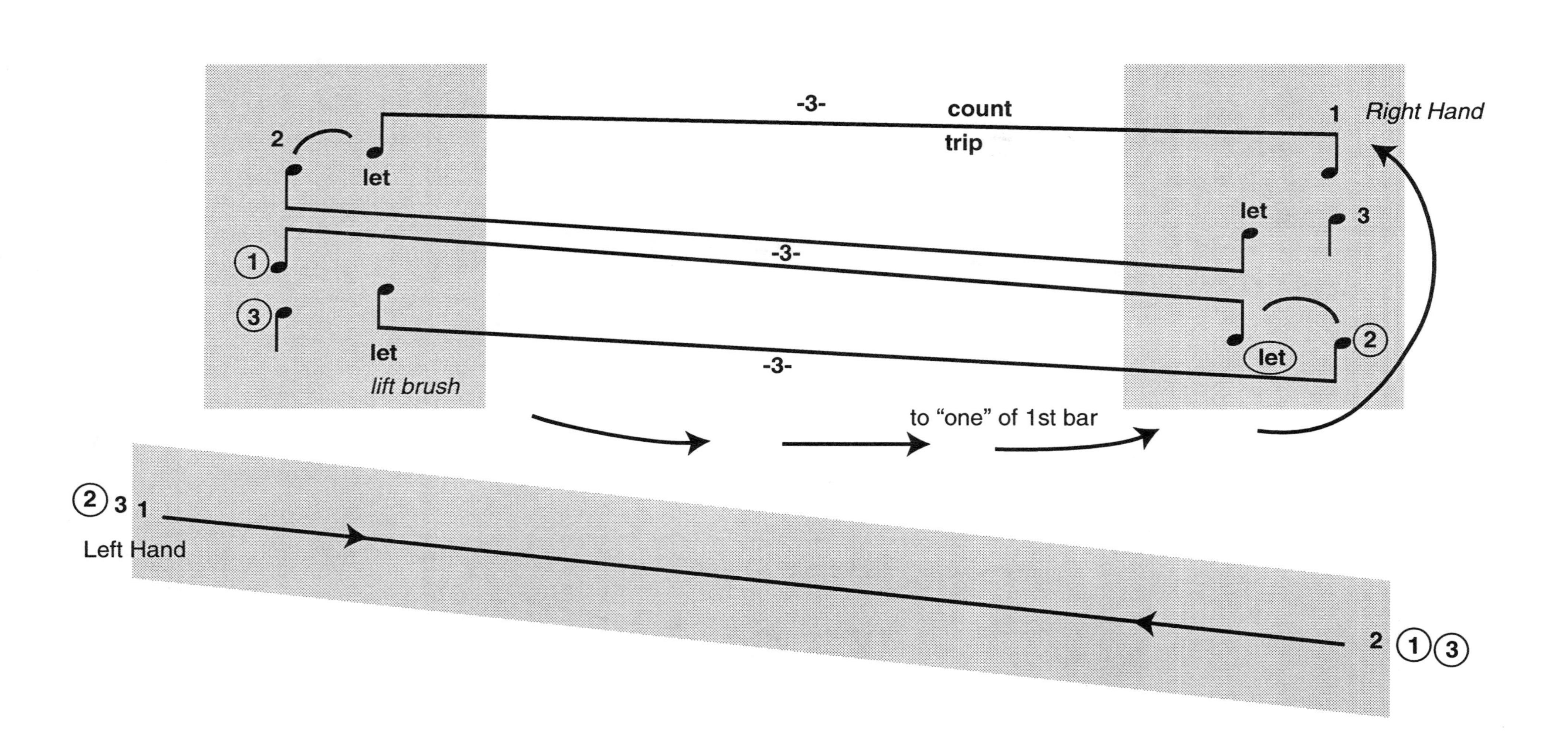

Note: The function of this stroke in 3/4 time is the same as it is in 4/4. Circled numbers represent alternate measures.

Sixteenth-Note Triplet in 3/4 Rhythm

Note: In 3/4 rhythm, the sixteenth-note triplet's starting point is reversed on alternate measures.

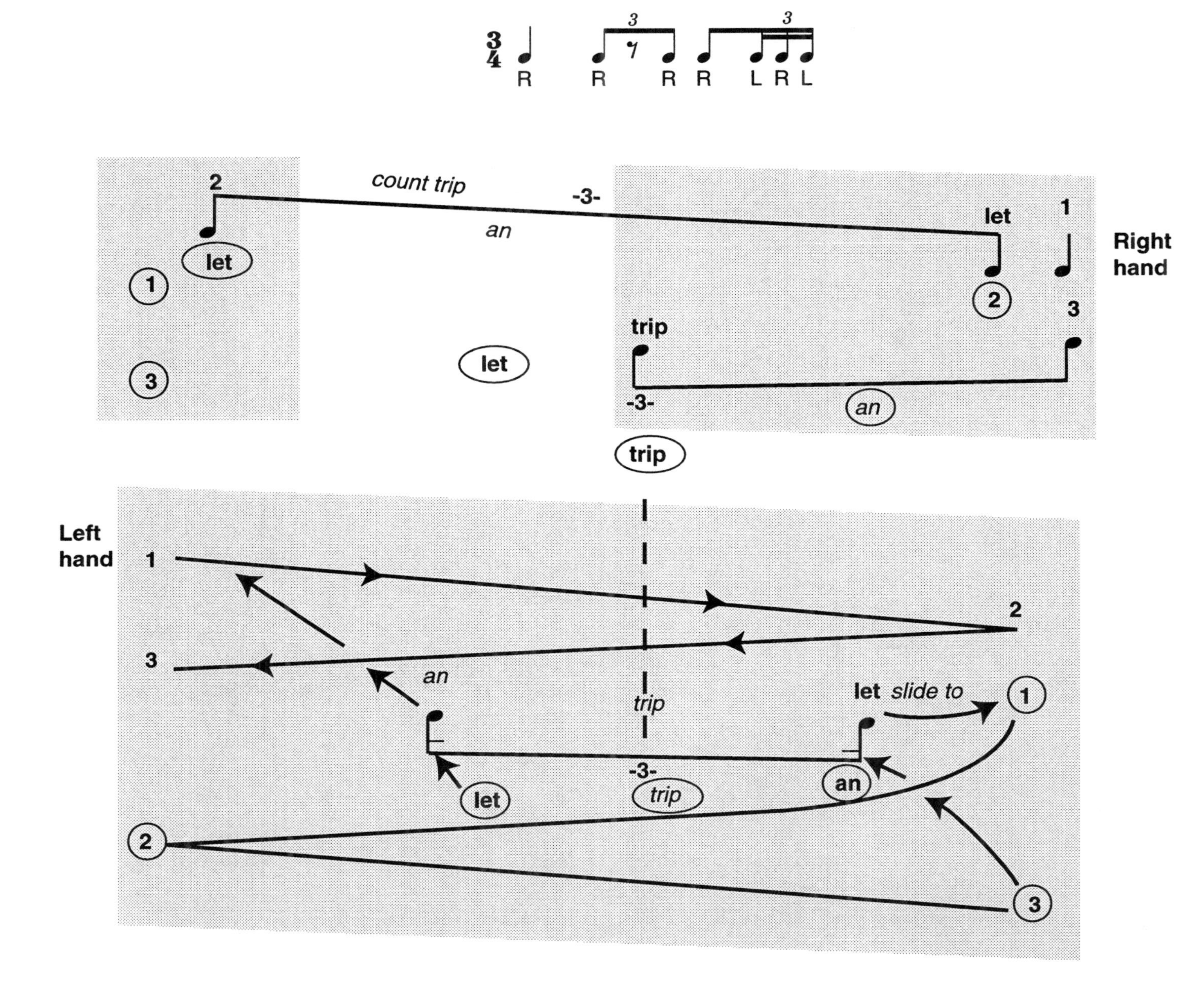

Sixteenth-Note Triplet Punctuation

The sixteenth-note triplet is used quite often as a variation of the altered triplet for punctuation. Remember that it comes on the count of "an," an-triplet, to be precise. Start the "an" count with the left hand. This stroke uses less area of the drum head.

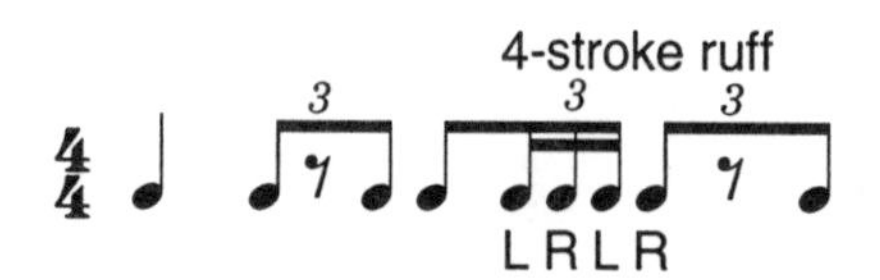

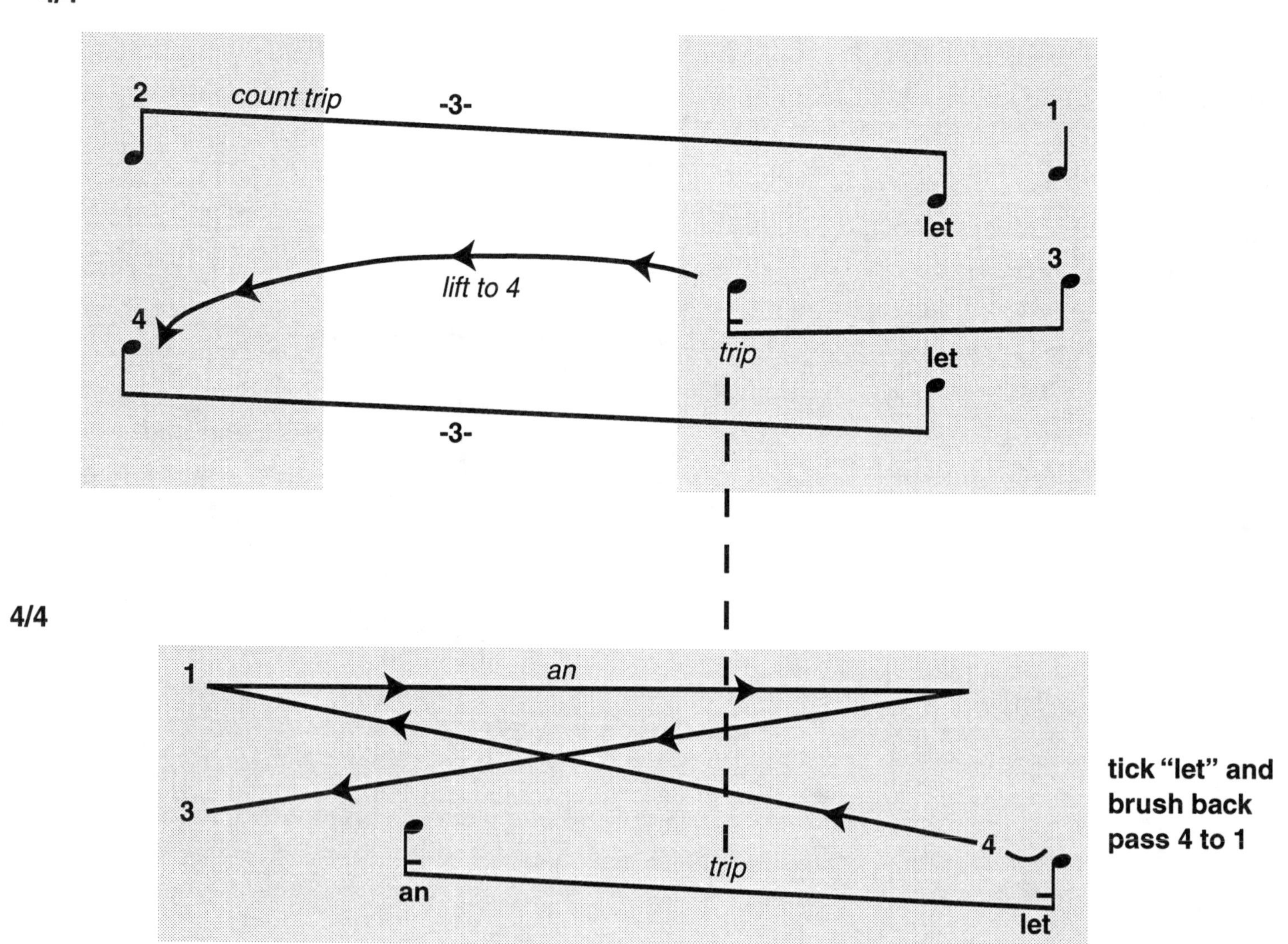

Stroke for Double-Time Feeling
(Ballad to Medium Tempo)

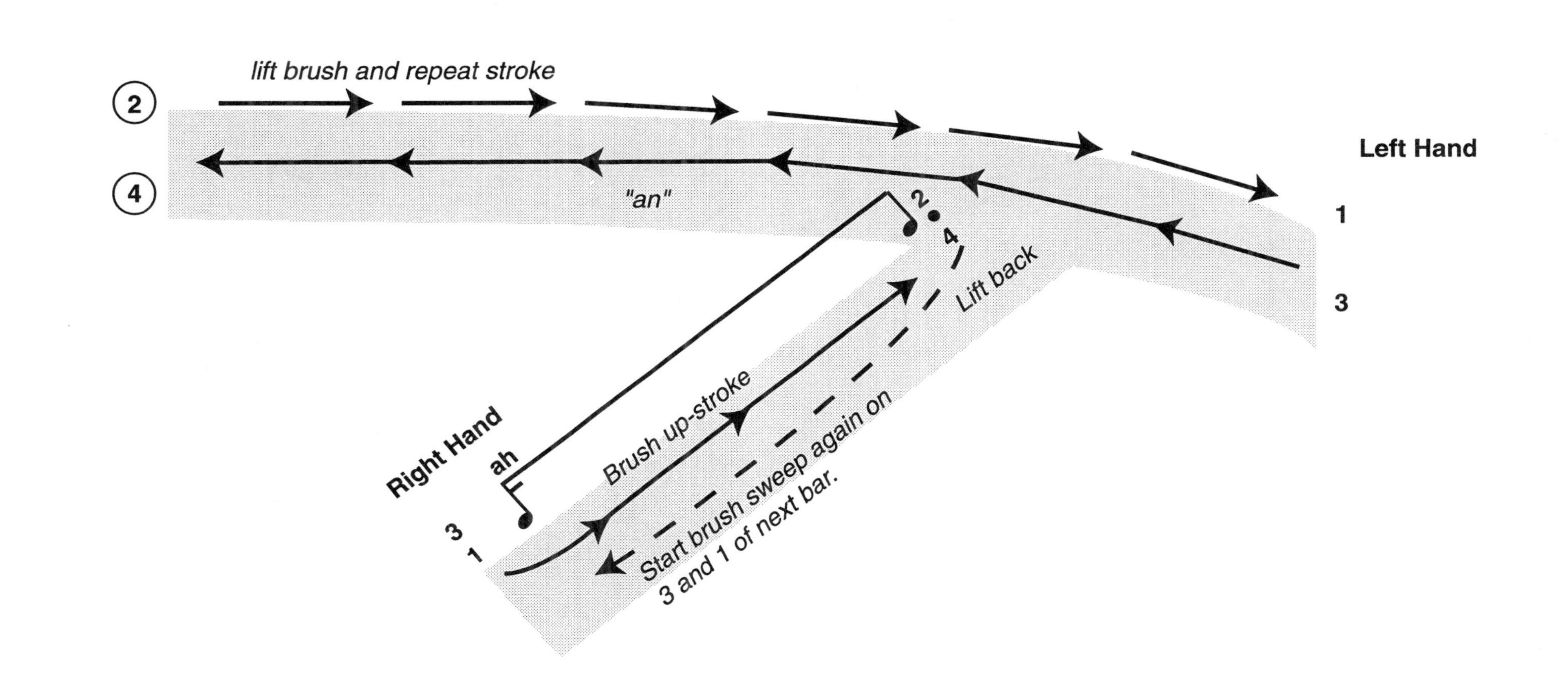

Note:
If you think and count in either eighth or sixteenth notes (1 an 2 an 3 an 4 an, or 1, 2 e an ah, 3, 4 e an ah) while retaining the basic 4/4 pulse, the double-time feeling will be realized.

Altered Triplet Shuffle

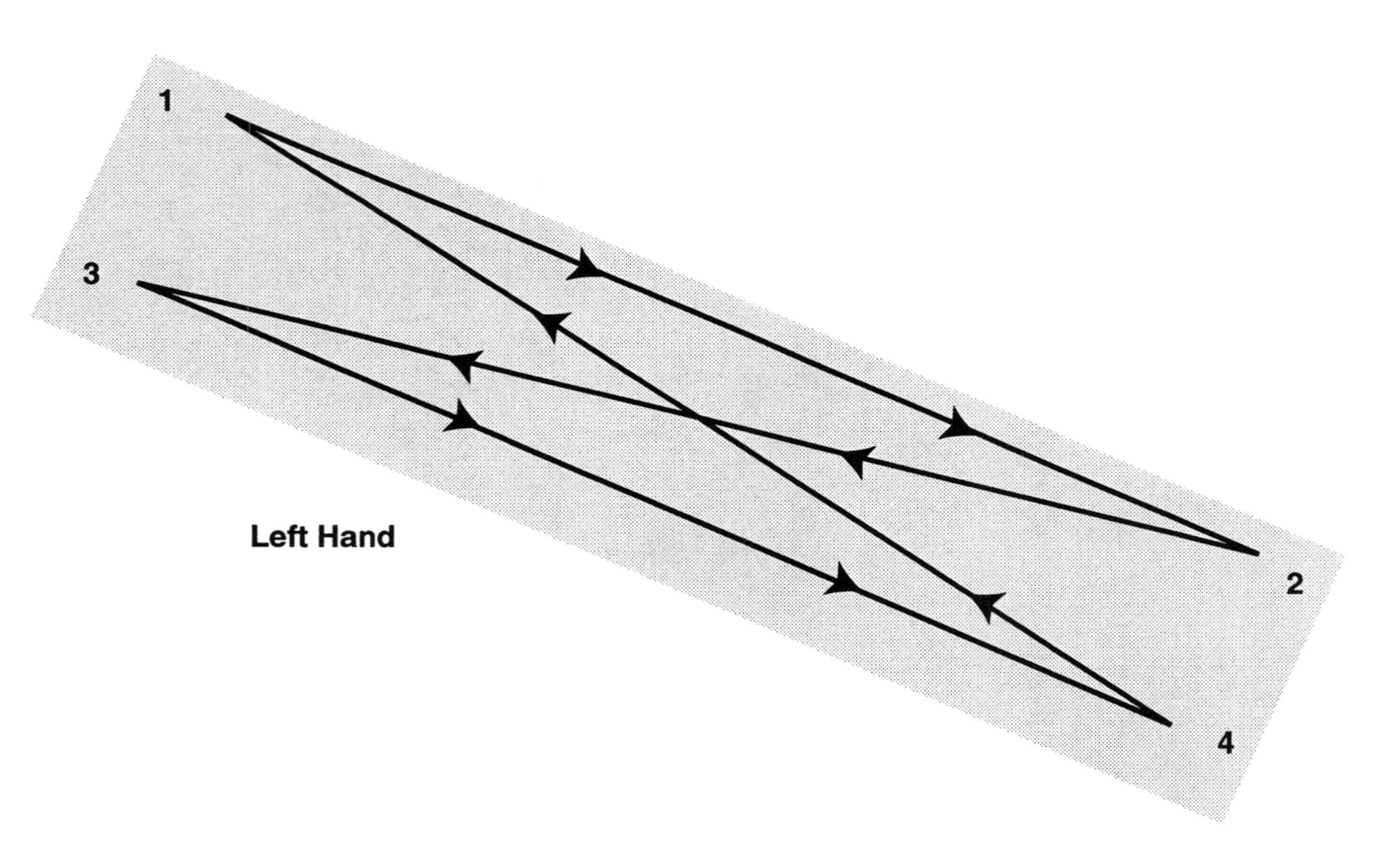

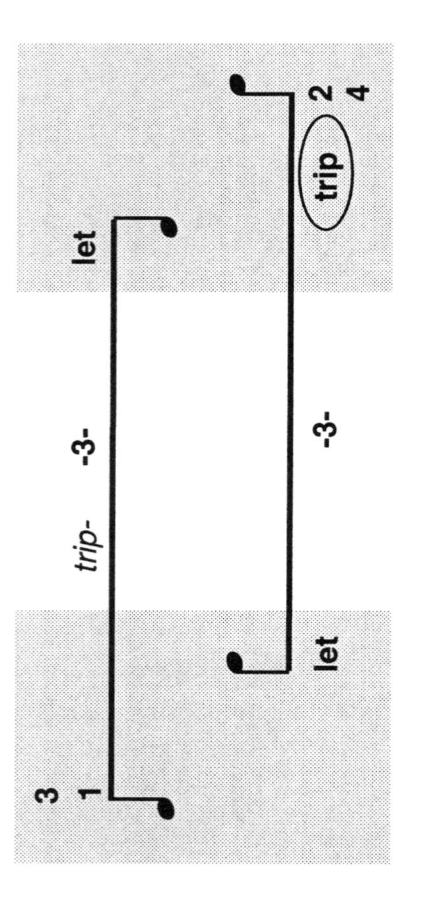

Tight Shuffle Sweep

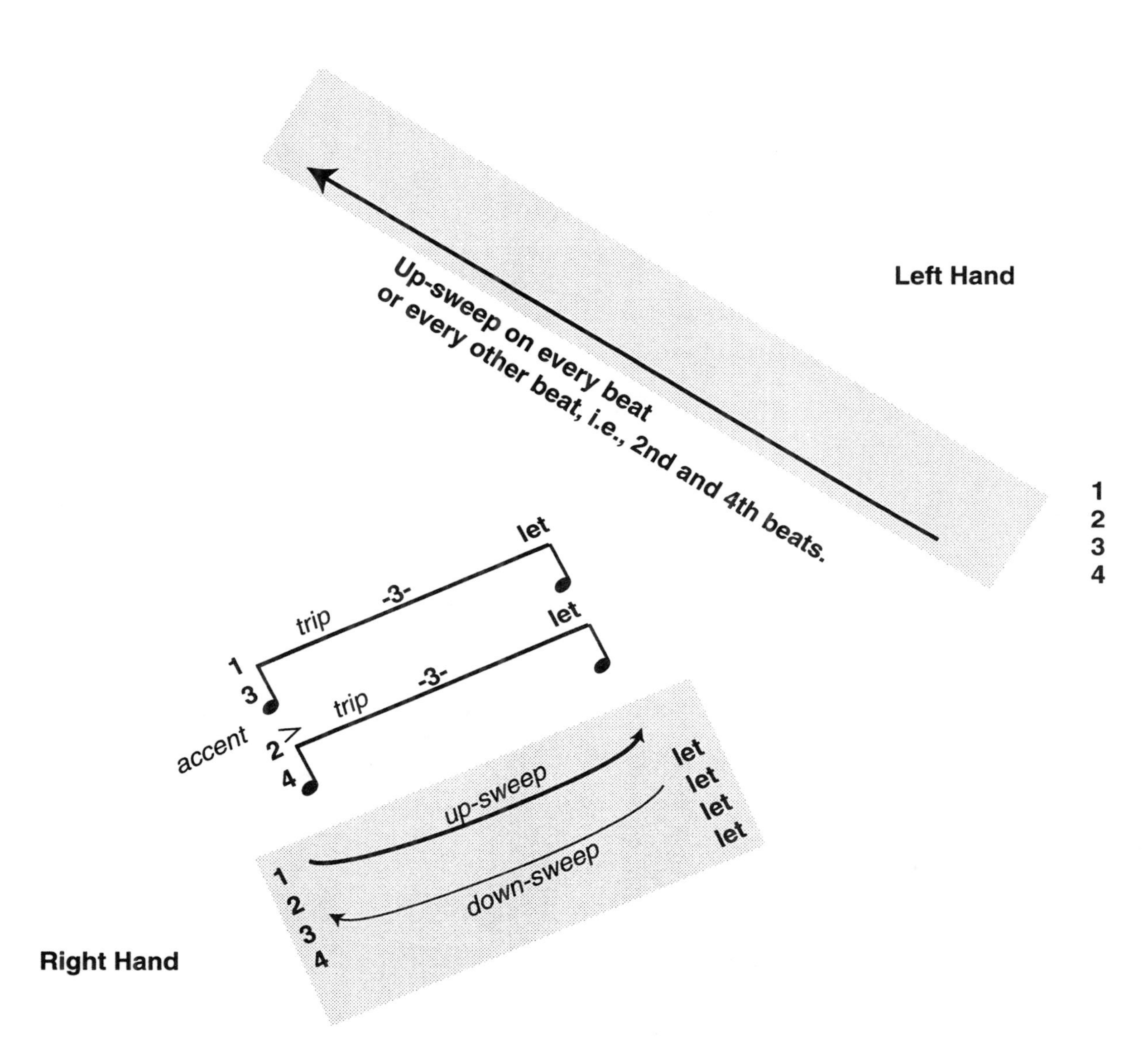

Brush Tap — Tick Brush
(Right and Left Hands)

Brush Tap - tick Brush
(Right & Left Hands)

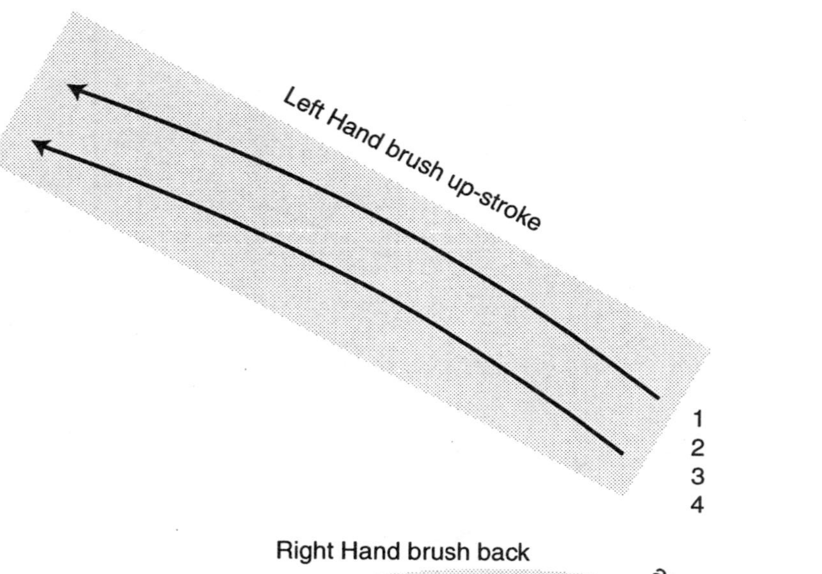

Left hand starts on the right side of the drum head.
Brush up and left on every beat or every other beat, i.e., 1st and 3rd.

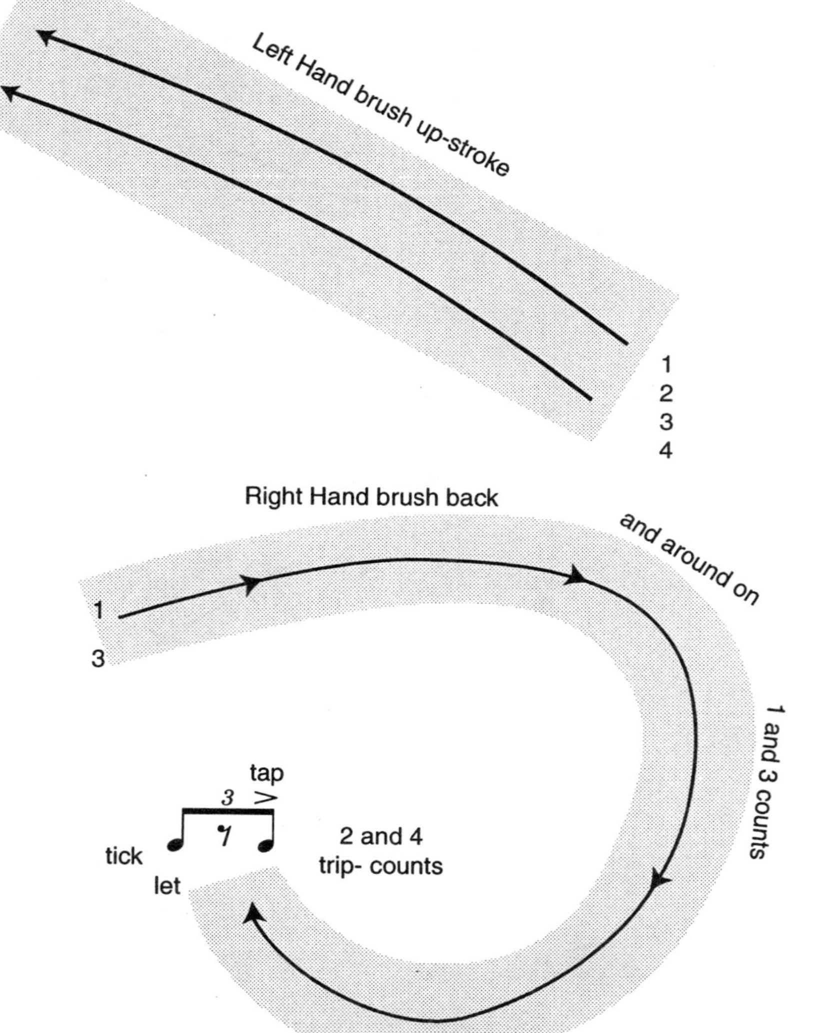

Right hand brushes left to right and curls around on counts 1 trip-let, then plays "tap-tick" on counts 2-let, brush back again on counts 3 trip-let and "tap tick" 4-let. Repeat.

Say, "Brush back curl T a p, tick, brush back curl T a p, tick," etc.

Strumming (Guitar Stroke)

When working with a rhythm guitar playing a straight four beats to the bar, or if you have no guitar and wish to get a light 4/4 rhythm guitar feeling, this stroke is very effective combined with the left-hand full circle.

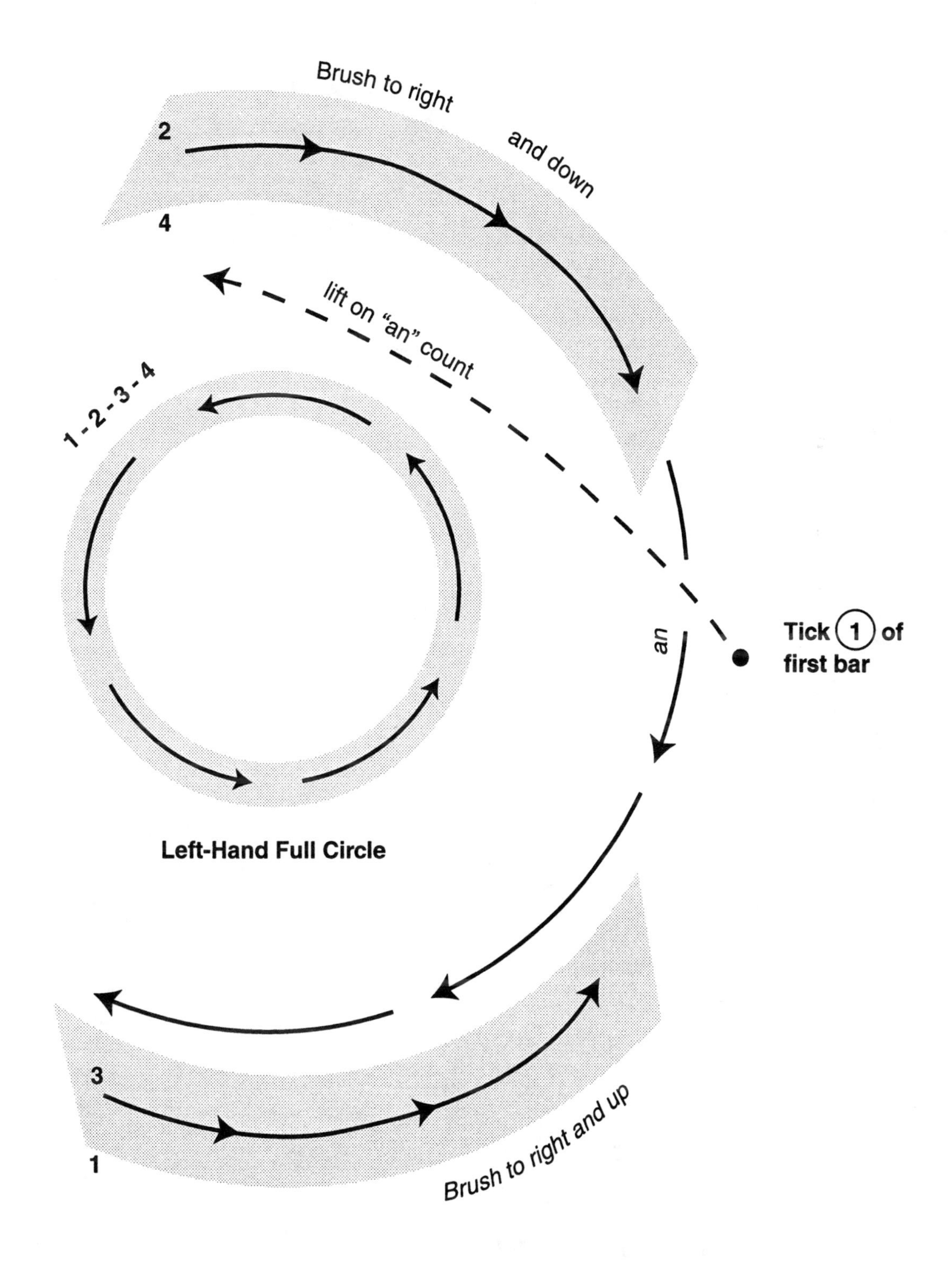

Note: The count "3" brush area becomes the count "1" area on alternate measures.

Tap-Sweep-Tap (Time Stroke)

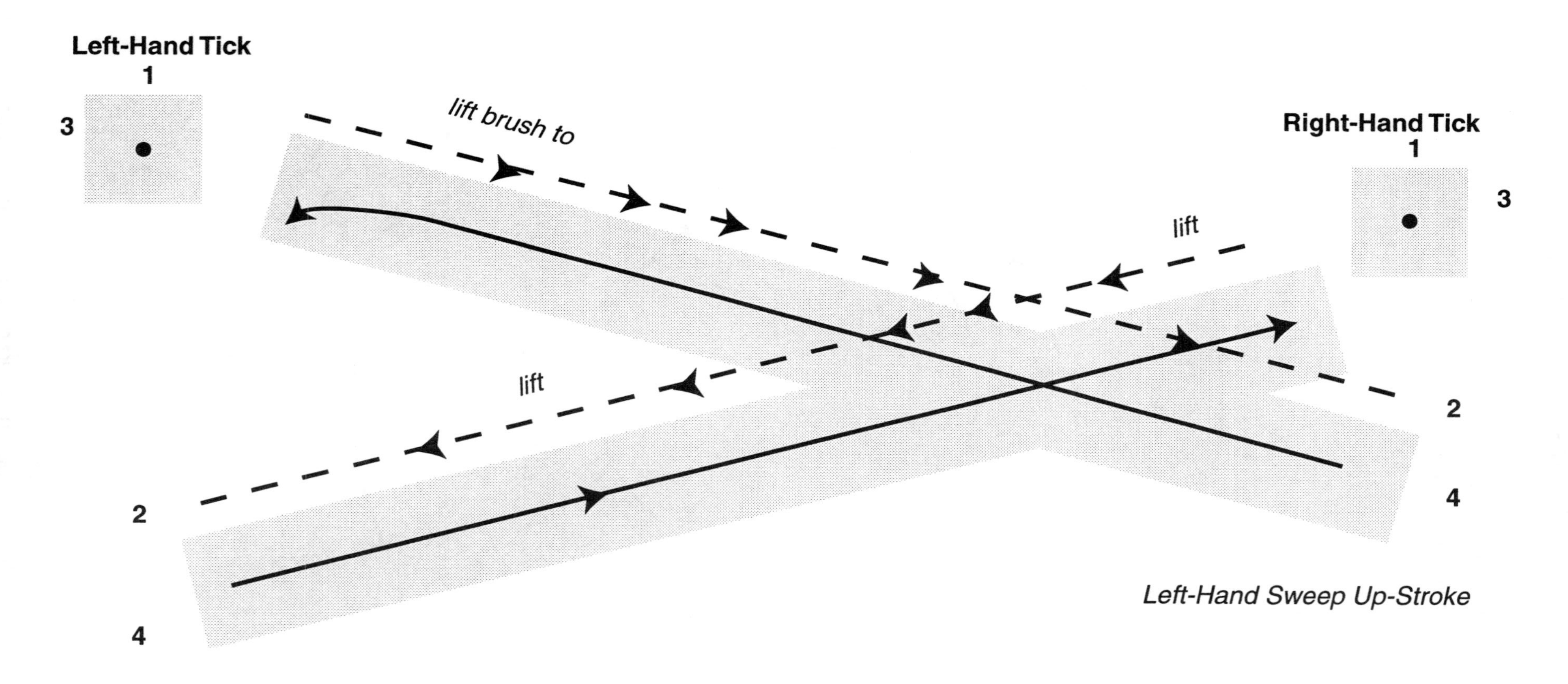

Dit-Dash, Dit-Dash, Dit-Dash

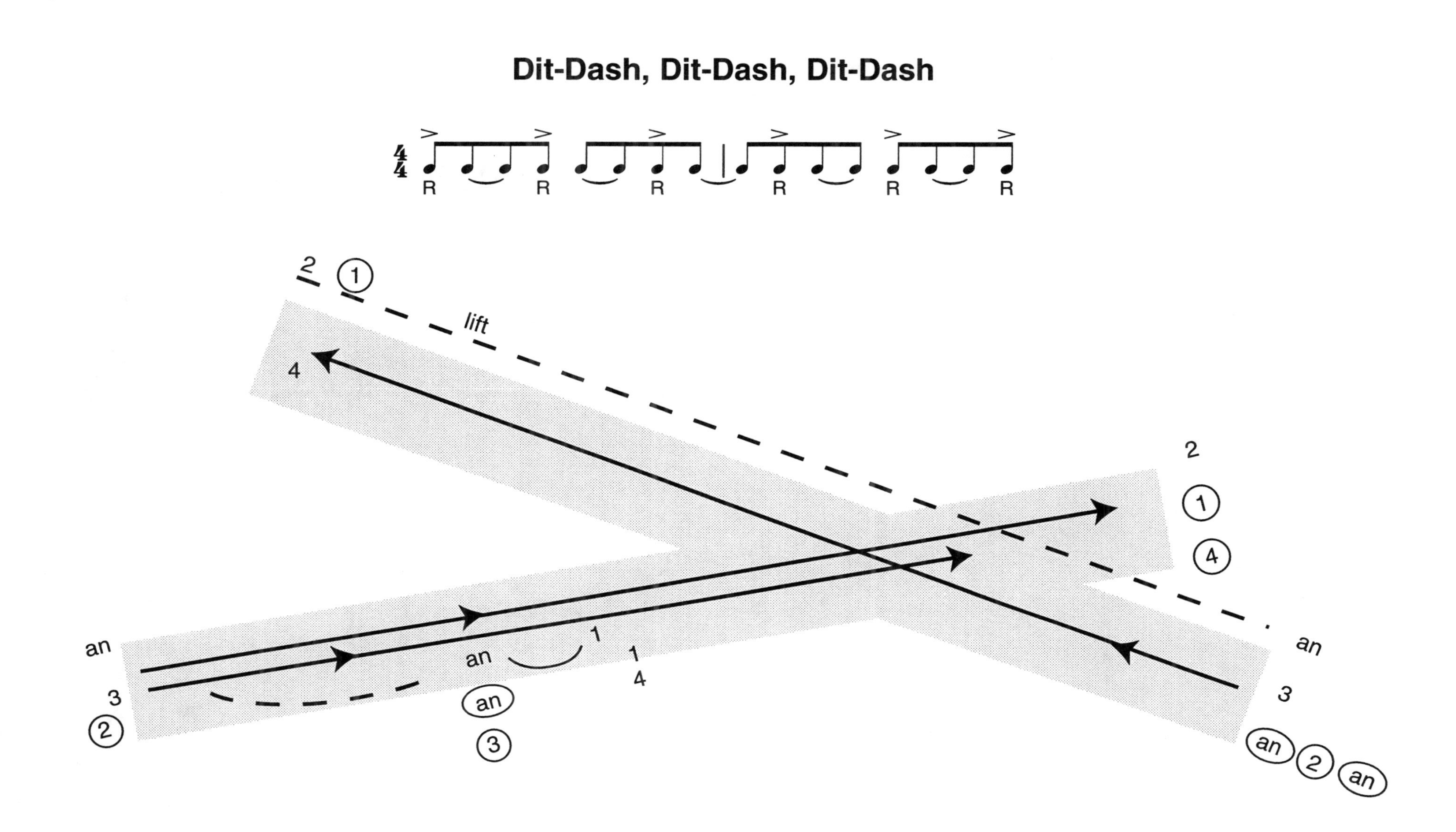

Adapting Brushes to Latin American Music

As mentioned earlier, brushes are very effective for soft playing. They can be used instead of sticks for playing Latin rhythms. For sambas and bossa nova tunes, the rhythm is frequently played with a brush in one hand and a stick in the other. The eighth- or sixteenth-note taps can be played with the brush while the other hand plays the basic bossa clave or other syncopated figures across the rim of the snare drum.

One can also simulate the sound of the scrapper or guiro by making long and short brush sweeps across the drum head. This sound can be quite effective, particularly when you don't have other percussionists in the group. Following are a few exercises to help you with these rhythmic sound effects.

I suggest that you trace these strokes with your finger tips before using the brush. Remember to do this very slowly at first.

Brush Sweep Exercises for Samba or Bossa Nova

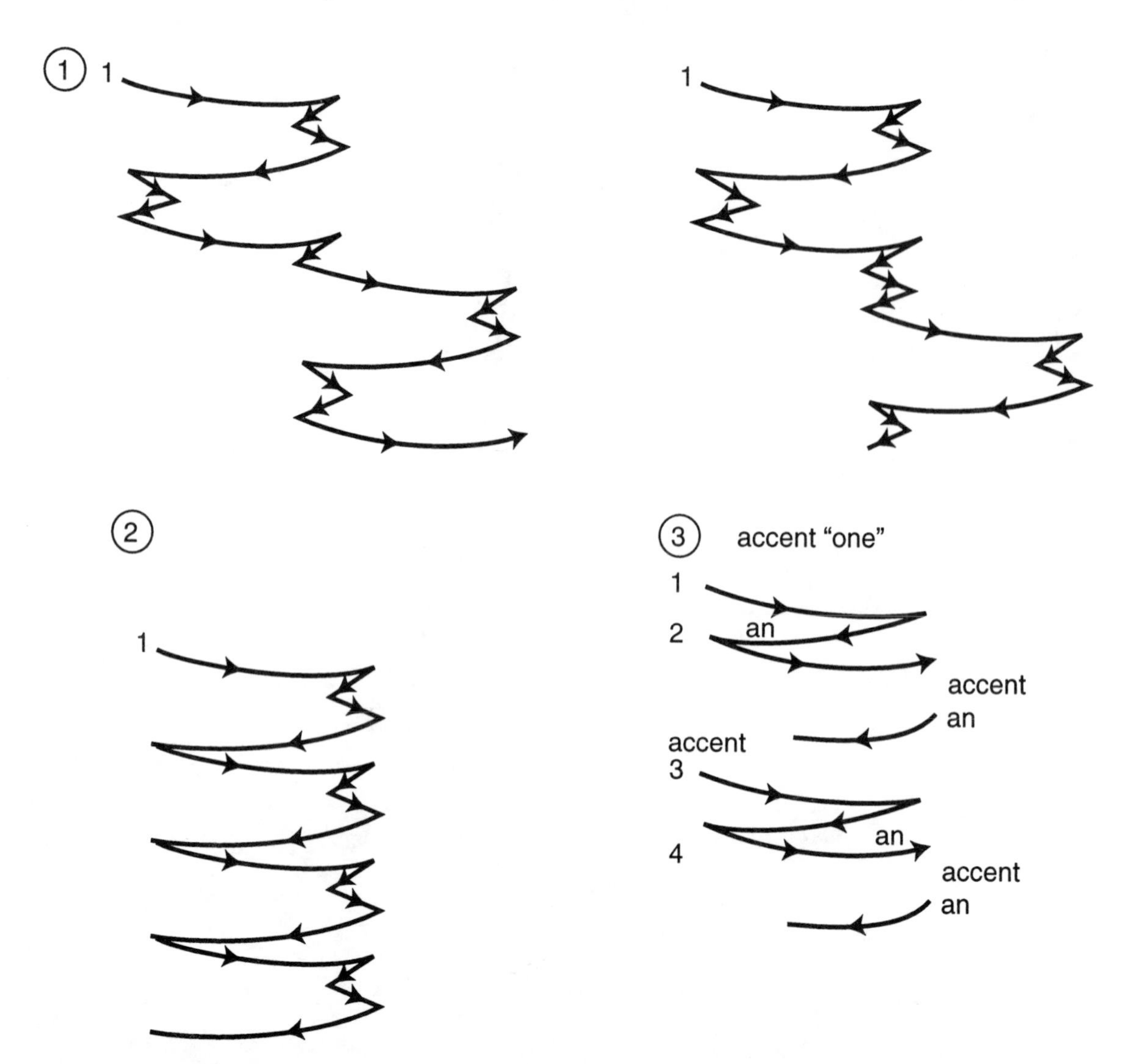

Notated Brush Sweep Patterns

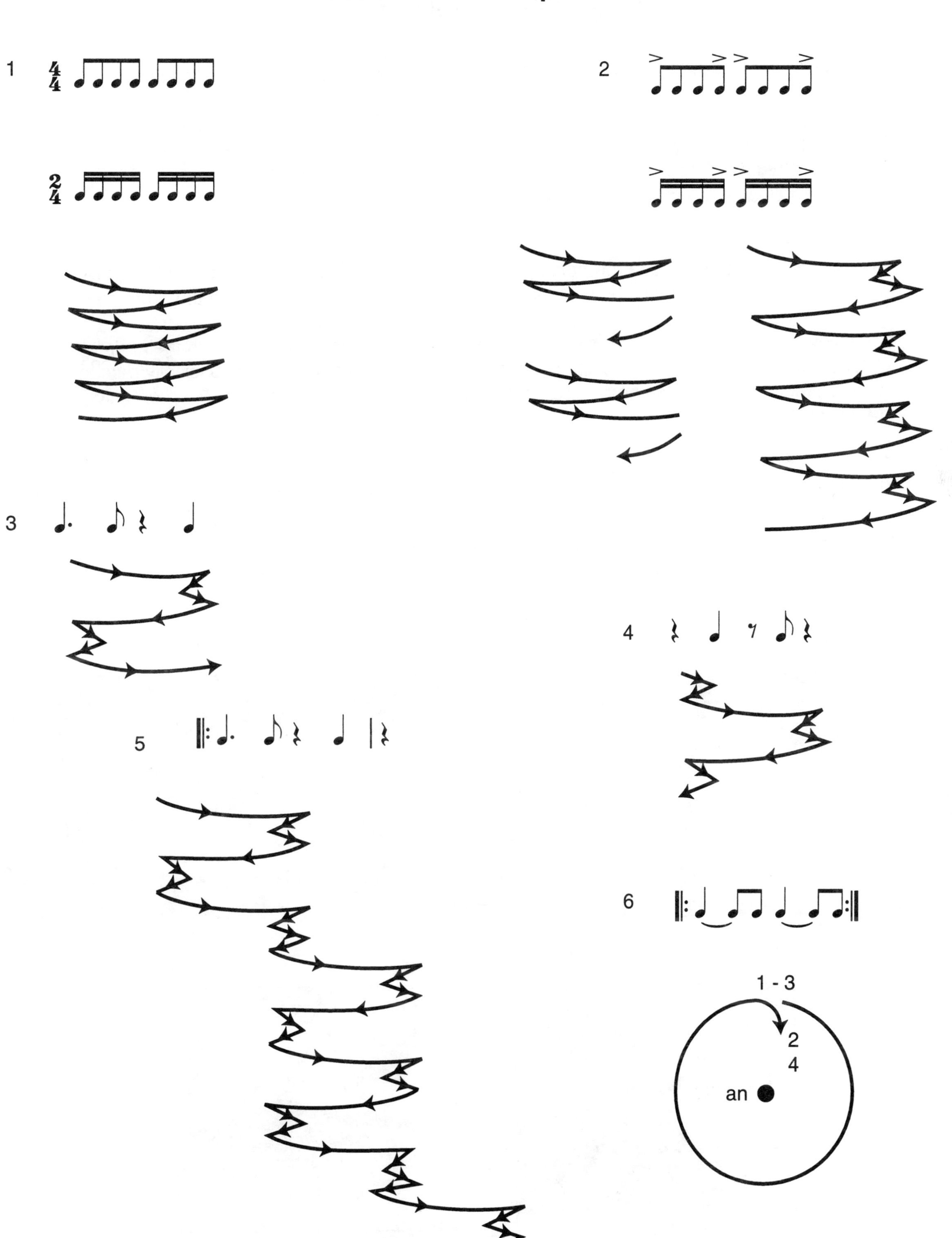

Single and Double Strokes

For practicing single and double strokes, the idea of the up-stroke is quite applicable.

One should try to play off of the drum head, so to speak, rather than down into it. This is accomplished by making quick down-up motions with the hand or hands, using the wrist as the natural pivot point for the hand. This is commonly known as wrist action. The result should be a clear, crisp "tick" sound from the drum.

Flat-Slap Sound
This sound is most often used for making accents or getting a heavier flat sound when playing rhythm. The slap is obtained by playing the brush flat and more down into the drum head.

The following exercises are very basic; however, practicing these exercises with their related stickings should help you in developing more than adequate technique. It is basically a good habit to practice all of the same rudiments, stickings, solos, and so forth, that you normally practice with sticks.

The use of the open square and the dot or filled circle will indicate which hand is to be used. The open square is for the right hand and the dot or filled circle is for the left hand.

It is also advisable for the drum-set player to practice all exercises while maintaining a steady 4/4 pulse with the bass drum, adding the hi-hat on the second and fourth beats of each measure. Try the same exercises using the hi-hat on each pulse beat.

*Note new Ed Thigpen signature wire brush

open retractable

wood clave, samba, bossa nova, effects

maximum flex

rubber mallet effect

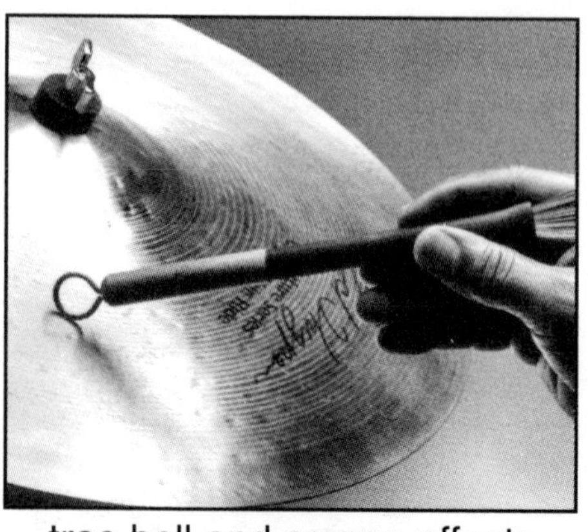
tree bell and scrape effects

Key

□ R.H.

● L.H.

Single-Stroke Exercises

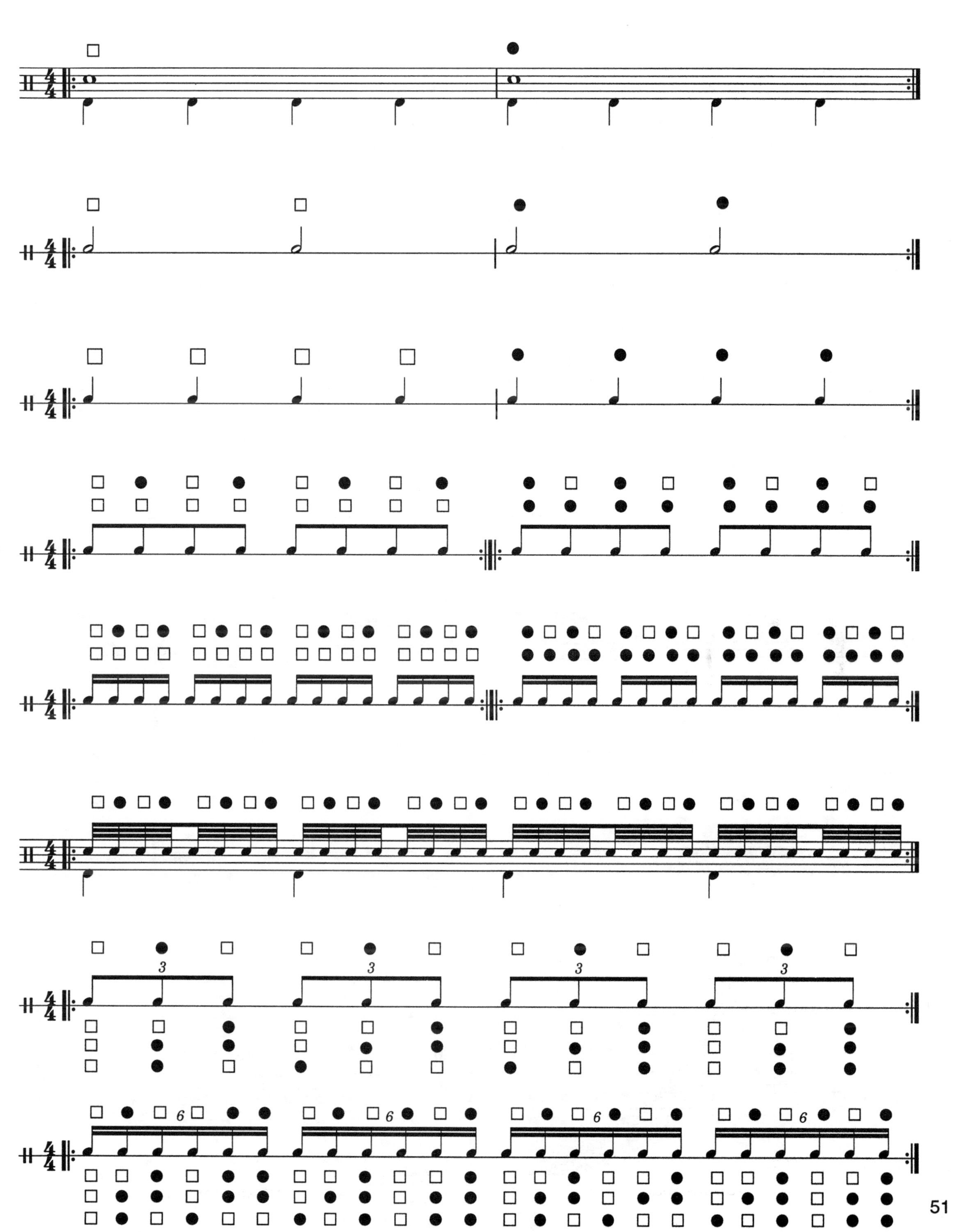

Key

□ R.H.

● L.H.

Double-Stroke Exercises

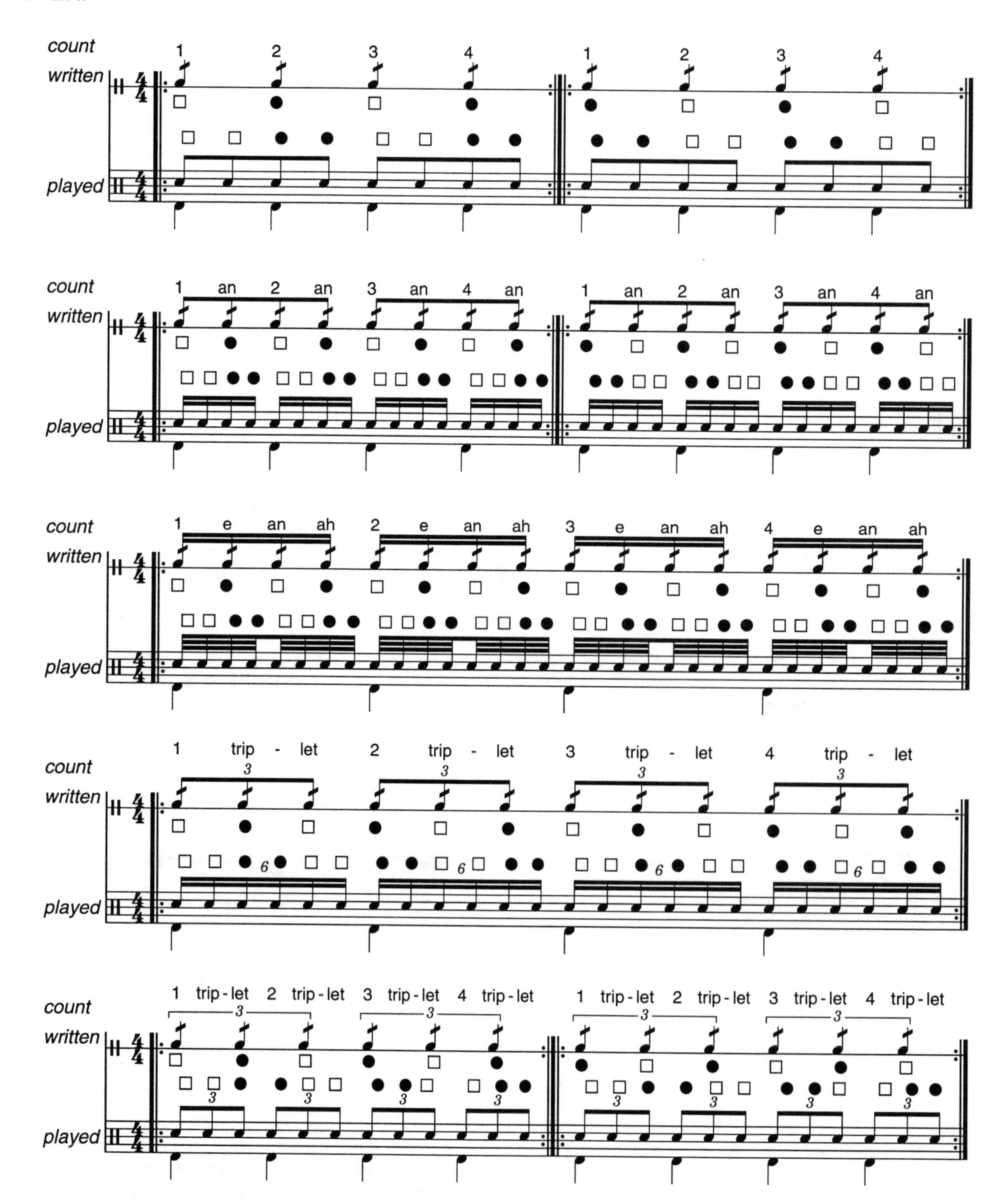

Key

□ R.H.

● L.H.

Flex and Multiple-Bounce Strokes (Wire Brushes)

When playing fast double or multiple-bounce strokes (three or more beats with each hand), making use of the natural flex or vibrations of the wire brush is necessary.

The flex stroke is executed with a quick downward wrist action without the up-turn, as with the single and double strokes. What happens is that instead of turning the wrist up again after the downward movement, you tighten or squeeze more on the brush handle and follow the vibrations of the wires downward with the hand.

With practice, you can control the amount of bounces, getting two, three, four, or more bounces with each single movement of the hand.

Multiple-Bounce Exercises

1 2 3 4 1 2 3 4

□ □ □ □ ● ● ● ●

1 an 2 an 3 an 4 an 1 an 2 an 3 an 4 an

□ ● □ ● □ ● □ ● □ ● □ ● □ ● □ ●

1 trip - let 2 trip - let 3 trip - let 4 trip - let

□ ● □ ● □ ● □ ● □ ● □ ●

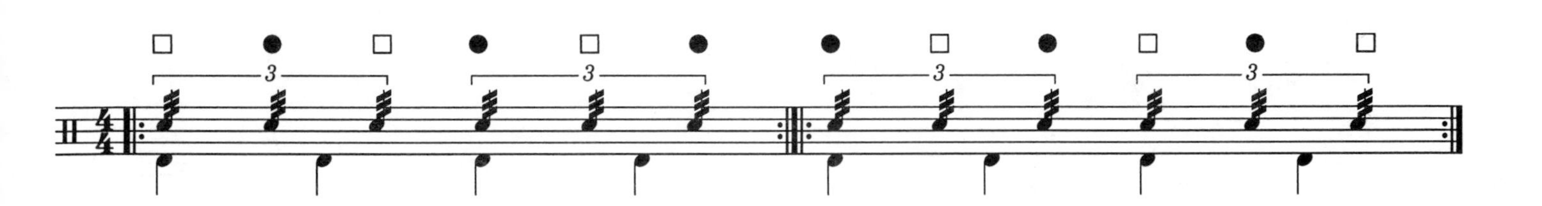

The Ed Thigpen
"Alt" Model Brush

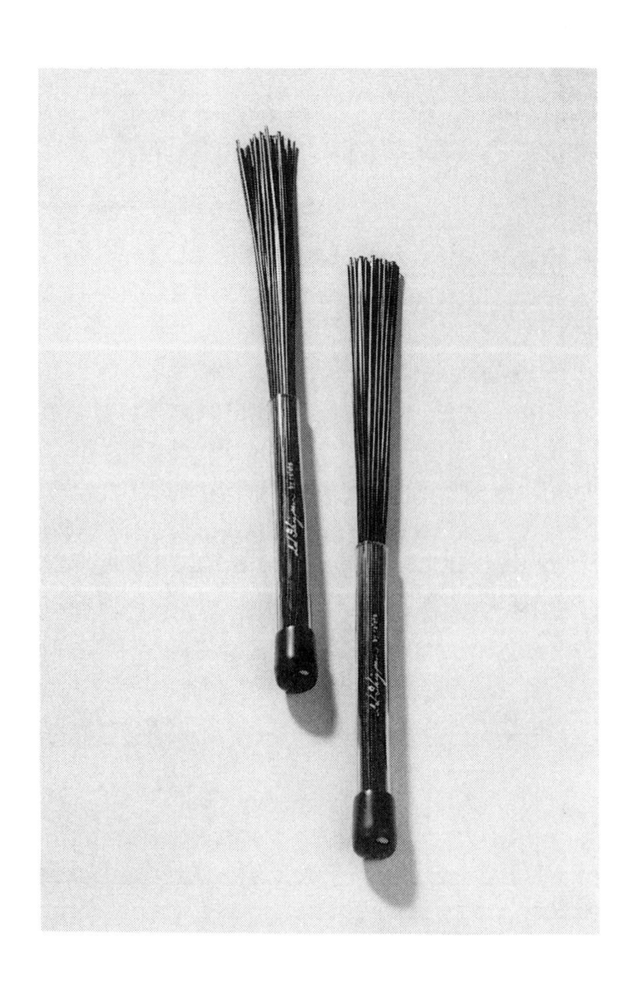

The E.T. Alt Model Brush is designed and constructed to give one an alternative sound and feel source.

The brush can be used quite effectively for playing Jazz, Latin, R&B, Country, and Rock rhythmic patterns on the drums without worrying about bending the wires. One can really dig into drums as well as play off the heads: (up-strokes). This is one of the reasons this brush has become so popular with rock & fusion players.

The sound and dynamic levels produced can range from a whisper to a roar. The handle on the brush as constructed absorbs and cushions the shock from hard hits on the drums.

Try the following exercises for starters, then proceed to practice rudiments, or any other stroke combination and patterns you would normally play with sticks or conventional wire brushes.

Single Strokes with Accents

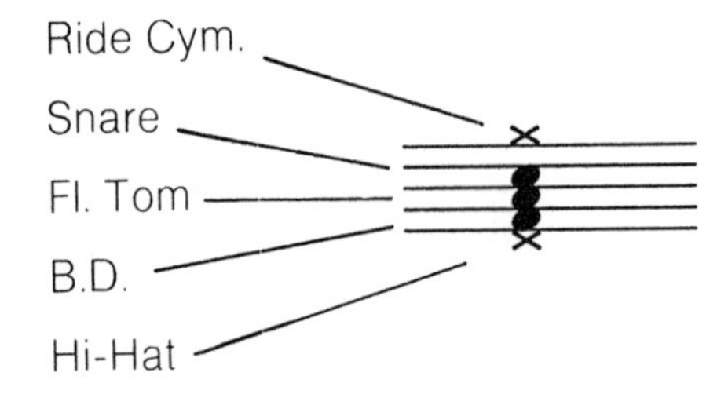

Practice each of these hand motion sequences when playing the following straight eighth-note pattern written on the snare drum space.

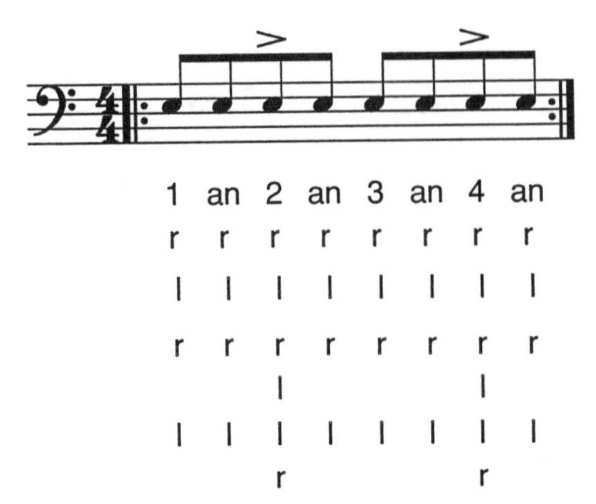

Practice with right hand only.

Practice with left hand only.

Right-hand straight eighths:
add left hand on counts 2 & 4

Left-hand straight eighths:
add right hand on counts 2 & 4

Funk/R&B/Fusion Patterns for Brushes

Practice all patterns with various stickings. Here are a few examples:

Funk/R&B/Fusion Patterns for Brushes (continued)

4/4 Grooves

8/8 Grooves

The use of accented sixteenth-note patterns played first at a moderate tempo can easily be adapted to a double-time feel by simply adding an accented hi-hat played on the "an" counts. Try applying this system to all of the 4/4 sixteenth-note examples.

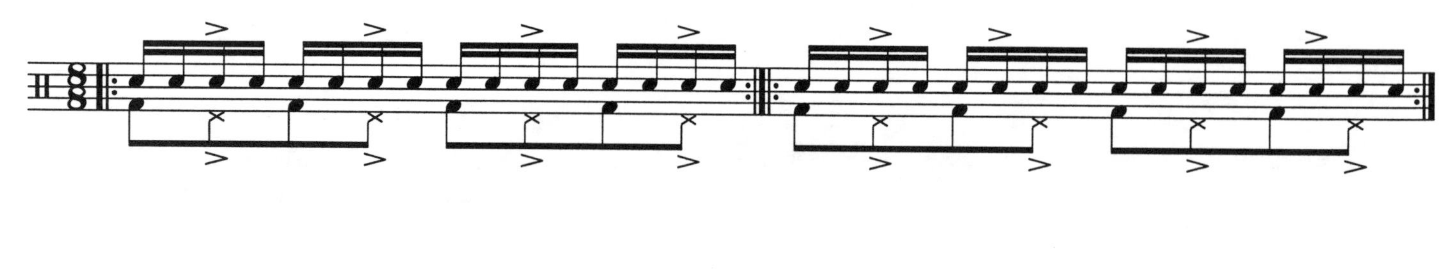

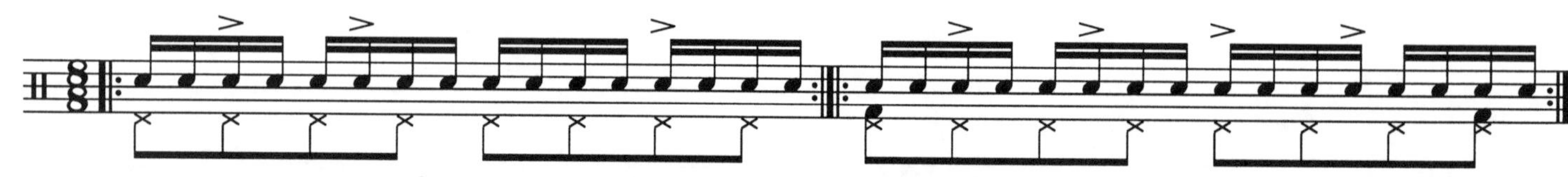

Artists' Comments

Here's what a few master drummer/percussionists have to say about *The Sound of Brushes.*

Butch Miles:
"Too often brushwork has been ignored as much as possible by students and teachers alike. Naturally, this has resulted in some pretty bad brushwork in this day and age. Ed Thigpen has called upon his vast knowledge and written a book that should be included in every drummer's library, be he student or teacher, novice or professional. It's time someone wrote a definitive book on brushes, and I believe Ed Thigpen has done just that. Thank you, Ed!"

Billy Cobham:
"After speaking to Ed Thigpen and listening to the accompanying recording, I've come to the conclusion that *The Sound of Brushes* is an essential element in everyone's educational library. Put it in the section marked Percussion, Traps, Contemporary. Try it! You'll like it!"

Harvey Mason:
"I would like to endorse your book [because] I feel that it is a great teaching aid I would use for students. Brushes are totally ignored by so many young drummers today; [therefore,] I feel that your book is even more valuable and should be exposed. Good luck with it, and I hope it's a hit!"

Carmine Appice:
"I want you to know that I think *The Sound of Brushes* is a great book for today, and I would recommend it for any students interested in learning today's brush methods. The recording is great, too!"

Jeff Hamilton:
"This is the most complete brush book written."

Billy Higgins:
"Truly a good book from one of the masters of the drums. I recommend this book of a lost art that is very important."

Jack De Johnette:
"Ed Thigpen's *The Sound of Brushes* book is a must for every serious drummer who wants to become a well-rounded musician in the music business."

Tony Williams:
"Ed Thigpen is the greatest and *The Sound of Brushes* proves it!"

"Papa" Jo Jones:
"After knowing Ed for lo, these many years, I can say that with his experience, this book on the sound of brushes I recommend."

Vic Firth:
"An articulate, progressive, well-organized approach to brush playing. An absolute must for any serious drummer."

Reviews

From *Crescendo Jazz*
The Sound of Brushes "Revised Edition"
Book/CD Review

For as long as I can remember, Ed Thigpen has, with only a handful of others, held the top seat in the art of brush work. In my estimation, he now scores very highly as a writer, although this is not his first book. Ed takes you step by step through many varied techniques. Also taken into account are the different types of handles and wires for producing a wide range of effects and tone colors. Right-hand punctuation, left-hand half and full circles, strokes for double-time feeling, flex and multiple-bounce strokes, and adapting brushes to Latin American music are just a few of the items included in this book.

At this point, I would add that the music of the accompanying CD is essential. The CDs are well done and clearly narrated by Ed personally, and without haste. Nowhere along the way does the student feel he is being rushed from one exercise to another. On the contrary, I found Ed to have a very relaxed way of talking, which reflected on the listener. I would recommend, as the author himself does, to listen through each example at least once without playing along with it and at the same time following the illustrated diagram visually. Also trace the diagram with your finger tips only. Take it stage by stage and allow yourself plenty of time. Well written and recommended for all levels.

From *Modern Drummer*
The Sound of Brushes
by Ed Thigpen

"Ed Thigpen is the greatest, and *The Sound of Brushes* proves it," raves Tony Williams; "Thanks to E.T. for giving us a book with a definite approach . . . ." says Max Roach. We tend to agree.

The Sound of Brushes is possibly one of the most enlightening books on the subject, written by a leading exponent of the art. Brimming with diagrams and directions. Thigpen has assembled a valuable yet complex reference, which demands concentration. The accompanying CDs are not only helpful—they are essential! An eye-opening look at a nearly lost art, by a true artist. Bravo, Mr. T!